The Real Northern Pow

The Industrial Revolution in the N

John Daniels, Dr Stafford M. Linsley, Alan Morgan, and Ken Smith
with photographs and images by Dr. Tom Yellowley

© Tyne Bridge Publishing, 2015

ISBN: 9781857952230

Illustrations © Newcastle Libraries/Dr Tom Yellowley unless otherwise stated

Published by:
City of Newcastle Upon Tyne
Newcastle Libraries
Tyne Bridge Publishing, 2015
www.tynebridgepublishing.co.uk
Design: David Hepworth

Cover: *Lemington Iron Works, 1835.*
Page one: *Newcastle, early 1840s, from Gateshead, showing the Brandling Junction Railway. The coal wagons are being pulled up an inclined plane from Redheugh.*
Contents page: *Undated image of workers and locomotives at Spencer's Steelworks, Newburn.*

Contents

Maling's Ford A Pottery, looking down Ford Street towards Byker Bridge, c.1878.

Introduction: the Industrial Revolution

In my simplistic view of the world, the Industrial Revolution began in 1709, when Abraham Darby, manager of the Baptist Mills brass foundry in Bristol, discovered how to smelt iron using coke rather than charcoal. This meant that iron could be produced more quickly and more cheaply, as long as coal supplies were plentiful.

Darby moved to Coalbrookdale, Shropshire, built his first blast furnace in the wooded valley, and began to make iron cooking pots. Other ironmasters followed, and soon Coalbrookdale was the iron-making capital of the country, if not the world.

One problem was that the increased demand for coal meant that the coal miners had to dig deeper below the water table and the mines filled with water, and flooding became a problem that could not be sorted with buckets, or horse-powered pumps.

Luckily Thomas Newcomen, ironmonger from Dartmouth, produced the world's first useful (atmospheric) steam engine in 1712. He built it at the Conygree Coalworks, near Dudley, in the West Midlands, and it soon solved the flooding problem there. There is not much hard evidence, but the second Newcomen engine may well have been built near Newcastle, where coal mining was a major industry, and flooding was becoming a major problem.

The Newcomen engine was not very efficient; mainly used in coal mines, where fuel was available nearby. It was an enormous beast, and needed a house of its own to keep out the weather. Each one cost about £1000, which was an enormous amount in the early 18th century, and yet they were so important that they were built all over the country, as well as being exported to France, Belgium, Spain, Hungary, Sweden, and even America. More than a thousand were built before 1800. So Darby and Newcomen between them put the Industrial Revolution into first gear. The many mine owners did not worry about the engine's thermal inefficiency given that it served its purpose of draining the mines of water.

In 1765, James Watt had the brilliant idea of installing a separate condenser to improve thermal efficiency. It took him ten years to get his first engine working, but after 1775 Watt engines not only drained mines but also powered machinery in the mills, and the Industrial Revolution moved into second gear. By about 1800, Britain led the world in the production of iron and steam engines, and with those advantages engineers felt they could do anything.

Meanwhile, failed wig-maker Richard Arkwright had invented a machine to spin cotton, and built a mill at Cromford in Derbyshire to house his water frame, with which an unskilled teenager could spin ninety-six threads at the same time. He had to borrow money to build the mill in 1771, but when he died in 1792 he left several mills, a castle in Derbyshire, a town house in London, and half a million pounds; so the water frame was a money-spinner too.

Inspired by his example, Leicestershire vicar Edmund Cartwright invented a weaving machine and the cotton industry took off in Lancashire. Soon it was said that half of all the world's cotton was passing through the docks at Liverpool.

Fiery Cornish wrestler Richard Trevithick began building high-pressure steam engines as soon as Watt's patent ran out in 1800. He put one of his engines on wheels, and created a steam-powered car which chugged up Camborne Hill in 1801, before catching fire while everyone was celebrating in the pub at the top. Then in 1804 he put a steam-powered vehicle on rails in the Taff Valley in South Wales, and to settle a bet, his steam locomotive pulled ten

Stephenson's locomotive Billy *(not Hedley's* Puffing Billy*) resident for a time atop the north end of the High Level Bridge (image c.1890).*

tons of pig iron (and seventy passengers) ten miles down the valley from the Pen-y-Daren iron works to the wharf at Abercynon.

Trevithick went off to South America soon after that, but in 1812 Matthew Murray, a Newcastle man who had moved to Leeds, built a rack railway to carry coal from the Middleton Colliery into Leeds; this was the first steam-hauled commercial railway in the world. The following year William Hedley, Jonathan Forster, and Timothy Hackworth, at Wylam near Newcastle built a steam engine locomotive, affectionately called *Puffing Billy*, for moving coal about the colliery.

In 1815, local mine-worker George Stephenson invented a safety lamp for the miners, and tested it in the most dangerous conditions. Humphry Davy also invented one in London, and there was a lengthy (and unnecessary) dispute about priority.

Inspired by *Puffing Billy* (and Murray's *Salamanca*) in 1814-16 Stephenson built a series of steam locomotives at Killingworth Colliery, and then in 1825, with his eighteen year old son Robert, built the Stockton & Darlington Railway. This was intended mainly to carry coal to the staiths at Stockton. On its first run, on 27 September, around five hundred people crammed themselves on the train, some sitting on piles of coal, and it achieved an average speed of eight miles per hour.

So Stephenson left the coal industry, and surveyed a railway route from Liverpool to Manchester. He was not a brilliant surveyor, and had to do it again to satisfy parliament, but luckily his son Robert, who had been to Edinburgh University and was a better engineer, designed the state-of-the-art locomotive *Rocket*. *Rocket* won the Rainhill trials in 1829, and the following year pulled the world's first dedicated steam-hauled passenger train from Liverpool to Manchester.

The Stephensons went on to build railways all over the north of England, and even from Birmingham to London, before George retired to Chesterfield. There he investigated various types of manure, and invented a cucumber glass, in order to grow straight cucumbers, thereby anticipating by about 150 years European Commission Regulation No. 1677/88, which said that Class I and Class II cucumbers must not be bent more than ten millimetres per ten centimetres in length.

By the middle of the 19th century the entrepreneurs of Newcastle were in full swing. William Armstrong invented a hydraulic crane, and the hydraulic accumulator, and the disaster of the Crimean War in the 1850s prompted him to design better guns for the British Army, and later better warships. He set up a factory on the banks of the Tyne at Elswick, Newcastle and expanded until he employed 20,000 people.

The need for electric light prompted chemist Joseph Wilson Swan to invent incandescent light bulbs, and working on his own in Gateshead he beat the world's most famous inventor to it. Swan demonstrated an effective light bulb to seven hundred people at the Newcastle Literary and Philosophical Society on 3 February 1889, and although Thomas Edison tried to sue him and put him out of business, he was eventually forced to go into partnership, and form the Edison-Swan electric Light Company, or Ediswan.

When Queen Victoria reviewed the Fleet at Spithead in 1897 she was astonished, if not amused, when Charles Parsons, in his steam-turbine demonstration boat Turbinia, ran rings round the ships of the Royal Navy and showed them where the future lay.

These few examples were far from the only industrial enterprises that flourished around Newcastle, and there is no doubt that the Industrial Revolution, which began in the 18th century in the West Midlands, expanded in the 19th century to make Geordieland the real Northern Powerhouse.

Adam Hart-Davis

The Industrial Revolution in practice: Wideopen, Newcastle

Wideopen is situated on the old Great North Road, five miles north-east of Newcastle-upon-Tyne. The discovery of coal here and the position of the village on a main route close to the industrial heartland of Tyneside, meant the area quickly became engulfed in the Industrial Revolution.

Work on Wideopen Colliery started in April 1825 with the sinking of the shaft, the first coal being drawn in May 1827. The colliery is described at this time, as having 'two shafts, contiguous to each other, for the drawing of coal, and another for the pumping engine; the depth to the High Main seam – which here averaged three feet, ten inches in thickness – is eighty fathoms, there is only one seam yet wrought here,' (Durham Mining Museum notes). The pumping engine was required to keep the deep workings dry by extracting water.

The exact year of this illustration is unknown but Thomas Hair's colliery sketches date from 1828 to 1842. Thomas Hair visited industrial sites – somewhere most people, unless they were employed there, would avoid – and made sketches of what he saw, providing us with an almost unique view of collieries in the North East at the time.

Something seems to have driven Hair to make these representations. Perhaps he was attracted by the business of colliery work, the complicated structures erected to extract the coal and bring it to the surface, then how this heavy material was transported from the colliery. This is not however, just about machinery and structures because his sketches are populated with the figures of colliery workers and pit ponies operating within this alien world.

The image provides us with an attractive general view of Wideopen Colliery from this early period. In the foreground, Hair shows a field with two horses in almost heraldic pose, while arranged behind are the colliery buildings, chimneys and pulleys and billowing smoke. By placing the horses, probably pit ponies, in the foreground of his sketch, Hair seems to be contrasting this rural presence with the industry behind.

There is a good deal of detail in the print that is not initially apparent. It is possible, for example, to make out the pitmen on the far right of the sketch, almost invisible against the hedge beside them, walking down the pathway to their shift underground. One man in particular stands out as larger than the others with corduroy trousers and large boots. He is followed by two boys, for in this period children were still working down the mines.

The real value of this illustration, however, is that it represents a particular point of time before some of the most dramatic changes associated with the Industrial Revolution take place. Directly in front of the colliery buildings a number of heavy coal wagons are shown with iron wheels running on metal track; the necessary components for a railway; only waiting patiently to pull the wagons away is a horse. Replace the horse with a locomotive and you have the railway as we know it, not just a system for taking coal from a colliery but a whole transport system.

It is possible to talk about a process of evolution; a series of stages occurring before a particular innovation takes place. It is unusual to be able to show this process, to have

Wideopen Colliery, drawn by Thomas Hair, this later etching by Davis.

Drawn by T. H. Hair.

the evidence for how things were just before the changes happen, how different elements come into place to make the change possible.

The process of change is perhaps inevitable, part of an evolution associated with the importance, from the earliest times, of coal in Tyne & Wear and the need to deal with this valuable, heavy substance once you have extracted it from the ground. It is this coming together of a number of elements that creates an opportunity, delivers a possibility that needs to be acted on. The engineer on the ground, faced with a practical problem, takes into consideration the different elements available and then comes up with a workable solution, the actual process of innovation.

George Stephenson working nearby at Killingworth Colliery solves these problems, developing a locomotive capable of pulling the coal wagons, at the same time as rails that can support their weight – not invention, more a question of adapting existing systems to the requirements of a specific situation. The form in which the solution to these problems first materialised can be seen in Stephenson's *Billy* at the North Tyneside Railway Museum, one of the earliest surviving locomotives – certainly used in just such colliery situations and possibly even at Wideopen.

Hair's visual representation becomes therefore of special importance. By choosing to place a horse pulling a series of heavy coal wagons in front of the colliery buildings, Hair is importantly showing the climate for change within the context of the colliery structures in which they occurred. Perhaps there is a locomotive just around the corner, already being used at Wideopen Colliery and that what is happening here is using horses for shunting purposes (horses remained in use in collieries well after locomotives were introduced). Thomas Hair, however, as he does elsewhere, would probably have wanted to draw the new locomotive, to include these brilliant new machines in his illustration.

An image of this kind, an illustration from the past, provides a privileged glimpse into how things were at a particular point of time. To go back to this same scene at Wideopen Colliery only ten or fifteen years later would probably show things as being much the same, with one central difference: heavy coal wagons would no longer be being pulled by a horse. The familiar culture of horse-drawn transport, a system in place from earliest times, steadily gives way to machines: locomotives capable of pulling a greater number of coal wagons and taking them much further than horses could ever manage.

What Hair provides in his view of Wideopen Colliery is an illustration of a problem needing to be solved, the situation as it occurred in collieries across the north-east coalfield and beyond. George Stephenson's locomotives solve this immediate problem but in the process open the door to a whole new attitude to transport, travel and distance, as railways burst out from the largely hidden industrial world to become a visible presence, powering their way across the countryside: the transport revolution, the most effective symbol for the extraordinary period of innovation and invention during the Industrial Revolution on Tyne & Wear that influenced the whole world

Wideopen, a community close to the centre of the innovation and invention associated with the Industrial Revolution might be expected to have in place a number of heritage features associated with this period, capable of acting as reminders of such an important industrial legacy.

As in many former colliery areas, there was a move at Wideopen to remove as swiftly as possible the unattractive pit heaps and remains of colliery buildings, associated with Wideopen and the later Weetslade Collieries – which closed in 1965. This however, was resisted, the distinctive high mound of colliery waste remaining as a visible presence, now transformed into the Weetslade Country Park, administered by Northumberland Wildlife Trust as a nature reserve.

The wagon way linking the mound of this former pit heap to the community of Wideopen still exists, one of a series of wagon ways formerly linking the different local collieries to the nearest docks and power stations. These have been made into a feature for cyclists and walkers by North Tyneside Council. It represents a significant local heritage feature, a surviving element from Wideopen's industrial mining past.

Certain measures need to be taken, however, before this heritage feature can achieve its full potential as a link to the past. The history central to the establishment of a heritage feature needs to be explored through information boards – Hair's illustrations providing a particularly suitable series of images for explaining the original appearance and history of the site and surrounding coal field.

In order for the location to become attractive, the surrounding environment needs to be improved, a place members of the Wideopen community – and visitors – are going to want to visit. Some landscaping is necessary with tree and shrubs planted, flower beds installed and benches positioned in sheltered locations.

A rather non-descript pathway can be transformed in this way into something special, a significant local heritage feature that helps give identity to the community, providing a direct link to its history.

Work is currently on-going with the Tyne & Wear Heritage Forum, Wideopen Local History Group; North Tyneside Council; Seaton Burn Community College and Bellway Homes to develop this project.

John Daniels

The image on the left shows the bottom of the shaft in Coronation Pit, Walbottle, the rollies have delivered the corves of coal in this etching c. 1840. The image on the right shows the image 'updated' to 1860, from W. Fordyce's The History of Coal, Coke and Coalfields *where tubs and a cage replace the rollies and corves.*

THE CHURCH PIT WALLSEND.

12   *Church Pit, Wallsend, 1830s.*

Coal

Although the Romans are known to have extracted coal in the North East, the history of coal mining in the region as a continuous organised industry stretches back to medieval times. Coal is known to have been mined in the Tyneside area as early as the 13th and 14th centuries.

From this period onwards the black diamonds were exported from the Tyne in small sailing ships that became known as 'colliers'. Much of the coal was carried south through the coastal waters of the North Sea to London. There it was known as 'sea coal' because it came to the capital by sea. However, the term may originally have been applied to coal collected after it was washed up on North East beaches from the undersea measures or where it outcropped on the shore.

Initially, coal was easily found on or near the surface and the first north east pits were extremely shallow by later standards. Among the early methods of extraction was the bell pit. These mines were simple affairs, a shaft was excavated to a depth of around forty or fifty feet and the coal was dug from the sides of the pit bottom. When it was unsafe to undermine the rock further because the overhanging roof was in danger of collapse, the pit, which by now was a roughly bell-like shape, was abandoned and work began on excavating another, often nearby.

Alternatively, if the coal outcropped on a hill or slope a short tunnel – known as a drift – could be started by digging horizontally or at a slight incline into the seam.

The black diamonds were mined both north and south of the Tyne. Coal even outcropped on Newcastle's Town Moor and was also found at The Forth, a green area outside the town walls. In 1239, Henry III granted permission to the Newcastle townsmen to dig for coal and over a century later, in 1351, Edward III granted permission for mining on the Town Moor and The Forth. The monks of Tynemouth are also believed to have mined coal and it seems that they may have shipped it from Prior's Haven, a small bay at the mouth of the river, from the 1260s onwards.

The importance of the industry continued to grow. By the mid-16th century a booming trade in coals had developed. This was a century of expansion for coal mining in the region. For example, in the year ending Michaelmas 1592, during the reign of Elizabeth I, a total of 91,420 tons was shipped on coastal routes from the Tyne, much of it going to the growing London market where coal was increasingly burned instead of wood to warm homes.

In earlier times wood had been the preferred fuel for home fires, with coal being used for industrial purposes such as lime burning and brewing, but by the Elizabethan period a shortage of timber brought about a gradual switch to coal. British forests were shrinking.

The amount of coal leaving the river continued to increase in the 17th century. For example, in 1633–1634 the total reached 452,625 tons.

As the higher deposits of coal were worked out, shafts were sunk to deeper seams. As the depth increased two major dangers were encountered – gas and water.

Methane gas, or firedamp as it is known to miners, led to numerous explosions in which large numbers of men and boys died. Added to this, carbon monoxide gas, known as afterdamp, could develop as an after-effect of an explosion and this led to further loss of life.

Other problems included chokedamp (also known as blackdamp) when there was a high level of carbon dioxide and very low level of oxygen in the air (sometimes present after explosions, but also occurring spontaneously), hydrogen sulphide gas, known as stinkdamp, and stythe gas, which occurs near the floors of workings.

Firedamp explosions frequently resulted from miners using candles or unprotected oil flames. Such naked lights were a great peril and Tyneside and County Durham were noted for their gaseous seams.

The deaths of men and boys as the result of the fatal combination of naked lights and methane gas led to the invention of the Geordie, Davy and Clanny safety lamps in the early 19th century. These lamps were designed to protect the flame from the explosive effect of methane but they gave a poor light and miners were still frequently tempted to use candles or unprotected oil flames because they were paid according to the amount of coal they could win from the seams.

As the pits grew deeper in the 18th century it was soon realised that an efficient system of ventilation was necessary to keep the air flowing through a mine so that 'foul' air such as methane gas and carbon dioxide was expelled and did not have time to build up.

An early method of ventilation involved equipping a mine with two shafts – the upcast and downcast. A fire was lit in a furnace at the bottom of the upcast shaft or suspended in an iron brazier in the shaft, thus expelling dangerous gases and at the same time sucking fresh air down the downcast shaft and into the mine. This kept air flowing through the workings. Sometimes the upcast and downcast airways were contained within the same shaft and divided by wooden partitioning known as bratticing.

However, a system of 'trap' doors between intake and outflow airways within the mine was needed to make the upcast and downcast system work safely and avoid the danger of gases building up in parts of the workings. Eventually, systems were devised that split the fresh air drawn into a mine via the downcast shaft between the working areas.

The 19th century witnessed the gradual replacement of the furnace method. From the 1860s onwards, large mechanical fans were introduced into pits for ventilation. These expelled the gases via chimneys, still using the upcast and downcast shafts system.

Flooding was another lethal peril for miners. Underground water might burst through at great pressure on to unsuspecting men from old, abandoned workings that had become flooded. Alternatively, workings could simply be 'drowned out' from water accumulated in layers of rock or sand seeping downwards, causing extensive flooding and resulting in closure of the pit.

Because of this, systems for pumping out mines were essential. Horse power to draw up buckets of water and later to work pumps was employed extensively in early pits, but was far from satisfactory.

A great step forward came in 1712, when Thomas Newcomen's atmospheric pressure pumping engine, which worked by means of a moving beam, was first used at a colliery. This engine was a much more effective way of keeping the water level down. Newcomen's engine enabled deeper seams to be worked in the North East. In the second half of the 19th century other, more efficient, pumping engines, worked by steam, came into use.

A major advance occurred in 1800 when Phineas Crowther, of Heaton, Newcastle, patented a vertical single cylinder winding engine and this eventually came to be adopted at many pits in the North East for carrying men and boys up and down the shaft, as well as bringing coal to the surface (bank). In the 20th century steam-driven machinery was gradually replaced by electrically-operated winding. However, steam machinery lasted at a few pits until the 1960s, and at Woodhorn Colliery in Northumberland until 1975.

In the 1700s and into the early 1800s miners had been raised and lowered to and from work on the shaft chain or rope. Alternatively, they might travel in a corve (coal basket) attached to the chain or rope. Such methods were, of course, highly dangerous and fatal accidents occurred.

A change in the containers for the coal led to an improvement in safety. By the 1840s corves were becoming a thing of the past and most North East pits were converting to tubs for transport. Tubs were small, box-like rail waggons that could be run from the coalface to an area known as the 'landing', where they would be linked together in trains, known as sets (see page 11).

From this point they were taken along the main underground roadways, or rolleyways as they were generally known, to the foot of the shaft bottom. The tubs were pulled along the roadways by ponies or, as the 19th century progressed, moved by wire rope haulage systems operated by stationary engines.

The introduction of tubs for the coal went hand in hand with the advent of the cage. Once at the shaft bottom full tubs were put into the cage for winding to bank. The first North East colliery to operate a cage may have been Woodside Glebe Pit at Ryton in 1835. Significantly, men and boys could now travel up and down the shaft in the much greater safety of the cage, instead of clinging precariously to a chain or rope.

Coal mining using horse power, c.1794. At the top of the shaft, a horse-gin for raising the coals, corves and waggonway horses can be seen.
(TWAM)

15

The Miners' Safety Lamp

In around 1813, Sunderland physician Dr William Reid Clanny devised a 'safety lamp' aimed at giving coal miners protection from the explosive effects of methane gas, or firedamp as it was known to the pitmen.

Born in County Down, Ireland, Clanny practised at the Sunderland Infirmary for many years. Despite his good intentions, his first lamp proved impractical.

Within two years other men were tackling the challenge. Killingworth Colliery, like many other mines in the North East, suffered its share of tragedies brought about by the 'fiery' nature of the coal seams. More than twenty miners were killed as the result of methane explosions at the colliery in 1806 and 1809.

Steam locomotive pioneer, George Stephenson, enginewright at Killingworth Colliery, had personal experience of these tragedies that took the lives of men and boys and it is not surprising that he should have turned his mind to the problem. Firedamp bedevilled the workings.

In August 1815, Stephenson began carrying out experiments to devise a safety lamp to protect miners from the gas. Some of these experiments took place down one of the Killingworth Colliery pits and involved carrying lighted candles near 'blowers'. These were fissures in the rock from which the methane (then often referred to as carburretted hydrogen) issued. Such experiments were, of course, extremely dangerous.

His eventual idea was to surround an oil flame with a protective glass cylinder and to encase this in a tin cylinder. Three versions of the lamp were produced, each one an improvement on the last. In the first version, air was allowed to reach the flame by means of a tube at the base of the lamp. In the third version, air was admitted to the tin cylinder and to the top and base of the glass cylinder by numerous small holes.

Meanwhile, in London the nationally famous scientist Sir Humphry Davy was also working on the problem and he too drew up plans for a safety lamp. Some of his experiments for the lamp were conducted in the North East at Hebburn Colliery. By coincidence, his lamp was identical in principle, although not in form, to Stephenson's. The truth is that both men had developed the same idea independently of one another. However, Stephenson had his lamp in use before Davy.

Davy announced his plan for a lamp at a meeting of the Royal Society in London in November 1815. The following month, Stephenson demonstrated his lamp, which became known as the Geordie Lamp after its inventor, at a meeting of Newcastle's Literary and Philosophical Society. But the Stephenson lamp was already in use at Killingworh Colliery. He had had it made by a Newcastle tinsmith and taken it into the mine in late October 1815.

Two years later, Stephenson wrote: 'This lamp was tried in Killingworth Colliery on October 21, 1815. The idea I had long entertained and the drawing was shown to several persons employed in that concern two months before the day mentioned, when I carried it with safety into a part of the mine where a strong blower of hydrogen was coming off. An experiment which was immediately repeated in the presence of two persons employed in that concern.'

The two men who accompanied Stephenson into the mine on this momentous occasion were his friend, apprentice viewer Nicholas Wood, and another fellow worker, under-viewer John Moodie. Modern research points strongly to the possibility that Wood contributed ideas towards the lamp.

Stephenson was clearly a man of considerable bravery. The methane could be heard hissing out from a crack in the rock. When Wood and Moodie heard the powerful blower they decided to go no further, but Stephenson pressed onwards. However, before he reached the spot

Left: *A collection of coal mining lamps.*

where the gas was issuing from the roof, the flame of the lamp went out but there was no explosion.

He then returned to his companions, relit the flame and moved towards the blower for a second time. On reaching it, he held the lamp directly in front of the escaping methane. Again, there was no explosion; the flame went out as before.

Stephenson returned once more to Wood and Moodie and he persuaded them to approach closer to the blower. He then repeated the experiment. For a third time, there was no blast. This emboldened Wood, who is believed to have held the lamp in front of the blower himself. All lived to tell the tale.

The Davy lamp, the flame of which was surrounded with a wire gauze, did not have a glass cylinder like the Geordie. Occasionally a draught might cause the flame from a Davy to pass through the gauze and make contact with gas. The Geordie, with its protective glass cylinder enclosing the flame, did not suffer from this defect.

In addition, the upper part of the Davy lamp was said to have a tendency to become overheated, another potential hazard in gaseous conditions. The Geordie's glass cylinder helped to prevent this happening. However, in around 1820 Stephenson redesigned his lamp, surrounding it with a gauze, similar to Davy's, but he retained the vital glass cylinder. Yet the Geordie was not perfect. One of its defects was that it could become dangerous if the glass was cracked or broken.

Dr Clanny, the first man to devise a safety lamp, went on to develop four more versions of his invention. The last version, brought out in around 1842, featured a gauze like Davy's, but the gauze was shorter and below it a large glass cylinder gave a relatively good 'window' for the light.

Other inventors in the 19th century developed improved safety lamps, but they all learned from the basic ideas of Clanny, Stephenson and Davy.

These lamps saved countless men and boys from death by warning of the presence of methane, the behaviour of the flame being a key sign. Yet the Geordie and Davy in particular gave a poor light for working at the face, and there is evidence of the emergence of the miner's eye problem, nystagmus, after the introduction of safety lamps.

Pit owners, believing in the efficacy of the lamps, sent men into more dangerously gas-laden seams and tragedies continued to occur, particularly in situations where candles were being used in a mine as well as safety lamps. The presence of the lamps could lull men into a false sense of security and firedamp could develop suddenly. The imperfections of the lamps subjected men to risk as did the use of gunpowder to bring down coal at the working place, where the fuses were lit by candles, and where ventilation was inadequate.

The lamps were by no means perfect, yet they continued to be used into the 20th century because they were superb gas detectors. Even after the introduction of the electric hand-lamp and cap lamp, mine deputies carried flame safety lamps for gas detection and around one in ten men also carried one.

The introduction of the safety lamp was not a straightforward affair, and some coal owners were roundly criticised for using early safety lamps as a substitute for truly effective ventilation. Improved ventilation was the main solution to combating the risk of explosions. This came from the 1860s onwards with the gradual introduction of powerful mechanical fans, driven at first by steam and later by electricity. Yet the flame safety lamp remained of vital importance for gas detection.

Ken Smith

An undated portrait of members of the Stephenson family. George Stephenson is holding a 'Geordie' lamp. The background shows a rural cottage, a steam train and a distant factory.

Shipbuilding

In 1839, Thomas Marshall launched a small iron-hulled paddle steamer, named *Star,* from his shipyard below the headland known as the Lawe Top at South Shields. She is believed to have been the first iron steamer built on the Tyne.

In retrospect, we can see that Marshall had taken a momentous step, for the Tyne was destined to become one of the world's greatest centres of metal shipbuilding. *Star* was a portent of a new era.

A wooden shipbuilding industry had existed on the Tyne for centuries. We know that a shipwrights' company was formed in Newcastle during the early 17th century and it is almost certain that the industry pre-dated this period. Shipwrights had the ability to construct as well as repair vessels and countless timber-built sailing vessels were launched from the river's banks

Wooden ships continued to be built into the 19th century, but by the 1840s change was under way. Iron could be shaped more easily than wood, and timber was increasingly in short supply as British forests shrank. These were two factors that were to attract ambitious men into iron shipbuilding. In particular, those with experience in the boiler-making trade were ideally suited to building such vessels because they were accustomed to working in iron.

Iron eventually give way to another metal. From the early 1880s onwards steel rapidly superseded iron as the preferred material for shipbuilding. The main advantages of steel over iron are its greater strength combined with less thickness, resulting in less weight.

In 1842, Thomas Marshall completed another pioneering iron vessel at his South Shields yard. She was the iron-hulled, propeller-driven steam collier *Bedlington*, the world's first steam collier. The *Bedlington* was employed on a coastal service carrying coal in wagons from the River Blyth in Northumberland to the mouth of the Tyne, where her cargo was loaded on to waiting sailing colliers. The *Bedlington*, which was over 135ft long, sailed on her short maiden voyage in September 1842.

Also occupying an important place among the pioneers of iron shipbuilding in the North East is John Coutts, who in around 1842 took over a former wooden shipbuilding yard at Low Walker on the Tyne. Coutts' first vessel, the 155ft-long iron-hulled paddle steamer *Prince Albert,* was launched in September 1842, the same month in which the *Bedlington* made her maiden voyage. The *Prince Albert* was to spend much of her useful life steaming up and down the Thames carrying passengers between London and Gravesend.

The year 1844 witnessed the launch by Coutts at Low Walker of the auxiliary steam propeller-driven collier *Q.E.D.*, which featured innovative water ballast tanks in the vessel's double-bottomed iron hull. Like many early steamships, she carried a considerable spread of sails and used her engines only when winds and tides were unfavourable or in calms.

Marshall and Coutts were pioneer shipbuilders in iron. The stage was set for the decline in the construction of wooden vessels. A metal shipbuilding industry was soon to rise to national and international prominence on this great river of the North East.

By the first decades of the 20th Century, the Tyne had established a worldwide reputation for turning out a great variety of well-crafted ships. These included passenger liners, cargo liners, oil tankers, ferries, warships and icebreakers. Added to this versatility was the skill and pride of its energetic workers.

Right: *Sail, steam and horse power on the Tyne.*

Charles Parsons and the Turbine Engine

The invention of the steam turbine engine by Charles Parsons, working on Tyneside, was a giant leap forward for civilisation, setting the stage for the cheap and efficient generation of electricity worldwide.

Charles Parsons was born in 1854, one of six sons of the Third Earl of Rosse, a noted astronomer. He was brought up at the family seat, Birr Castle in County Offaly, Ireland, and, under the influence of his father, became fascinated by science and engineering.

At the beginning of 1884 he became a junior partner in the ship equipment manufacturers, Clarke Chapman and Co., of Gateshead, and headed their electrical department. There he took the most significant step of his career by developing a steam turbine engine for driving a dynamo to generate electricity.

With great ingenuity and perseverance, Parsons overcame the extreme difficulties of developing this high-speed engine in which the force of steam is applied to the blades on a rotor. Parsons patented his turbine engine on 23 April 1884 and devised a generator to go with it. It was a massive technological advance.

The engine proved to be a complete success. Clarke Chapman began manufacturing steam turbo-generators to provide electric lighting in ships. The first vessel to be lit by the new equipment was the *Earl Percy* of the Tyne Steam Shipping Company.

The turbine engine was clearly a machine of enormous potential for the electricity industry. It was time for the inventor to move on. In 1889, he ended his partnership with Clarke Chapman. Together with friends, he formed a company, C.A. Parsons & Co., which set up a works at Heaton, Newcastle, and further developed and expanded production of turbo-generators.

Also in 1889, Parsons set up the Newcastle and District Electric Lighting Company, which opened the Forth Banks Power Station in 1890 to supply power to the West End of Newcastle. Two Parsons' 75-kilowatt turbo-generators were installed at Forth Banks – the first to be used at any public power station in the world.

In the same year, John Theodore Merz formed the Newcastle upon Tyne Electric Supply Company and went on to establish a power station at Pandon Dene to supply power to the East End of the city.

The city of Elberfield in Germany ordered two 1,000-kilowatt turbo-generators from Parsons' Heaton Works in 1901. A year later Parsons supplied two 1,500-kilowatt turbo-generators to the Neptune Bank Power Station at Wallsend, which had been opened in 1901. This station, which had superseded the one at Pandon Dene, was the first public supply station in Britain to produce three-phase electricity for industrial use.

The turbine machinery manufactured at the Heaton Works grew ever larger and more powerful and the Parsons Company established a national and international reputation for expertise in this field, supplying turbo-generators worldwide.

The inventor also adapted his steam turbine to propel ships at high speeds on the oceans and seas. He installed his marine steam turbines in an experimental boat, *Turbinia*, which was launched into the Tyne at Wallsend in 1894 and she underwent a long series of trials in the North Sea. During the first half of 1897, *Turbinia* clocked over thirty knots on these trials. The boat eventually achieved a maximum speed of around 34.5 knots, making her the fastest vessel afloat in the 1890s. She staged a spectacular display of her speed during Queen Victoria's Diamond Jubilee Fleet Review in Spithead, between Portsmouth and the Isle of Wight, in 1897.

The marine steam turbine went on to achieve great success and was installed in fast passenger liners and major warships from the early 20th century onwards. Vessels that were propelled by turbines included the famed passenger liner *Mauretania*, launched by Swan Hunter and Wigham Richardson on the Tyne in 1906 and completed the following year. *Mauretania* held the Blue Riband for the fastest crossing of the North Atlantic longer than any other passenger ship in the early 20th century. Her turbine engines were built by the Wallsend Slipway and Engineering Company under licence from the Parsons Company.

Charles Parsons, who was knighted in 1911, achieved a revolution in electricity generation and ship propulsion. He was undoubtedly one of the world's greatest engineers. Sir Charles died in 1931, aged seventy-seven.

Ken Smith

Turbinia *in the Tyne, 1894. Built by Brown and Hood at Wallsend.*

Transport

When the Newcastle & Darlington Junction Railway was formally opened in June 1844, the train-load of 'gentlemen' who reached Gateshead from Euston in just under nine and half hours, were part of a truly historic occasion, for never before in the history of the world had anyone covered three-hundred and three miles overland in so short a time. A few years later, Thomas Sopwith noted, after a ninety minute train journey from Brighton to London in 1852, some fifty miles, 'what magic – what annihilation of time & space'. For travellers more accustomed to road travel, when a journey from London to Gateshead might take the mail coach forty-four hours in good conditions, or twenty-five hours by the fastest horse-drawn coach available, the steam-hauled railway must indeed have seemed revolutionary.

But the trajectory of railway development in the UK goes back to the first decade of the 17th century, when Huntingdon Beaumont, a Leicestershire entrepreneur, built what became known as a 'waggonway', a horse-drawn, wooden-railed system, in use by October 1604 near Nottingham. He built another in the Bedlington/Blyth area in the following year. Both were designed to carry coal. The Bedlington venture did not last very long and was abandoned by 1616, but this was far from the end of horse-drawn waggonways in north-east England, the earliest to the Tyne was created in around 1621. For the next two-hundred years, horse-drawn waggonways were essentially used to carry coal from mines to navigable water, then to be shipped, primarily but not exclusively, for sale in the London markets.

By the 1620s, increasing demand for coal had all but exhausted the above-water seams near the banks of the Tyne and Wear, and consequently waggonways became more necessary, in preference to more expensive carriage by pack-horses or wains, for a wooden rail, set upon wooden sleepers, had a rolling resistance some one-third or one-quarter of that of an un-made road.

Even so, the take-up of the waggonway system, where one man, one horse, and a mainly wooden, four-wheeled waggon capable of carrying a chaldron (fifty-three hundredweight) of coal to staiths on navigable sections of the North East's rivers, seems initially rather slow; the Benwell Way of around 1627 was followed by the Stella Grand Lease Way, possibly before 1635, but certainly by 1653, and others in the Gateshead area by 1647 and 1659. These waggonways were all quite short, less than two miles long, but demand for coal after around 1660 led to a further expansion of the coalfield beyond the tidal limits of the rivers, and with waggonways up to three times longer than before; in these ways the great mineral and land owners were able to maintain their established markets. Not all was sweetness and light, however, for coal owners and landowners were frequently at loggerheads, primarily over the wayleave arrangements required to run a waggonway over land between mine and river.

The waggonway allowed a major hurdle to be overcome – the efficient carriage overland of high-bulk, low-value minerals like coal, and in thereby enabling new parts of the north-east coalfield to be opened up, the waggonway allowed coal outputs to be expanded to meet increasing demands. The cost of carrying coal for four miles overland, before railed systems, was about the same as carrying it

Next page, clockwise from top left 1) *A chaldron waggon of coal approaches the Tyne, the horse has a welcome rest as the gradient carries the load downhill.* 2) *A former waggonway at Horsegate Wood, Greenside.* 3) *A waggon on display near Causey Arch.*

over water from Newcastle to London, perhaps 320 miles. Quite simply, collieries up to about six miles from the navigable rivers of the North East needed waggonways to maintain their economic viability.

Consequently, horse-drawn waggonways continued to be built in north-east England, to the River Wear from 1693 for example, and were also built elsewhere in the country, sometimes being referred to as 'Newcastle Roads', almost always for the carriage of minerals to water. Some north-easterners also created waggonways abroad, for example, John Stafford from Newcastle, who became manager of a mine near Helsingborg, Sweden, (where John Watson, also from Newcastle, was viewer for a while) introduced a waggonway there in 1797.

The advantages of a waggonway were quite clear, but still, of course, they had to be engineered. As the aim of a waggonway was to enable coal to be carried to navigable water by the most direct route possible, the average gradient was downhill, and where the waggon could descend by gravity alone, the horse could simply trot behind the waggon. Seeing the 'cart put before the horse', was a sight that appealed to many visitors to the region.

Each waggonway, and its branches, was built by a particular coalowner, or group of coalowners, for their own purposes, and although hundreds of miles of waggonway were built in North East England, they did not provide, nor were they intended to provide, an integrated railway system. Moreover, there was a multiplicity of track gauges, between the Tanfield Way at four feet, and the Wylam Way at five feet.

Left: *Causey Arch, near Stanley is the world's oldest surviving railway bridge. It was built 1725-26.* Right: *The 'Dandy', Walbottle, photographed in 1909.*

Canal proposals and the turnpikes

Meanwhile, from the middle of the 18th century, turnpikes, river navigations and canals were being created throughout many parts of the country. But among the major industrial areas of Great Britain, only the north east of England never had a canal. However, given the spirit of the times, it is hardly surprising that a number of canal proposals, as well as schemes to extend navigation on its major rivers, were made for the North East, mainly to suit the coal mining and iron working areas in County Durham, and for the Tyne-Solway gap. Only the latter schemes had any real chance of succeeding, but their implementation was delayed, partly through a lack of consensus on preferred routes, until the Newcastle & Carlisle Railway was built and put an end to canal talk.

The turnpikes were a different matter – no part of the country came to be without its toll roads. Although a General Highway Act of 1555 made parishes responsible for the upkeep of their roads, a lack of technical knowledge, and possibly of enthusiasm for the work involved, resulted in less than satisfactory roads. Parish roads did not generally constitute elements of trunk routes, but where they did, maintenance was equally poor. Moreover, such roads were without guide posts or milestones, for parishioners had need of neither. 'Turnpike Trusts', the fundamental idea behind which was that road users should pay for road upkeep and for the creation of new roads by means of the tolls paid to travel along them, were seen as a remedy for such situations, but while these were encouraged by government, the necessary initiatives to create a Trust depended upon local interests and locally generated funds.

The first local Act for what came to be known as a 'turnpike' was passed in 1663, covering a southern section of the Great North Road, London to Edinburgh via Newcastle, and it is perhaps not surprising that the earliest turnpikes in the North East were along the same road. In the 1740s, and 1750s, the Great North Road was turnpiked, more or less progressively, through North Yorkshire, County Durham, and into Northumberland. Many important branches from this road were also soon turnpiked, for example by the Acts passed in 1747 for the Stockton to Durham road via Sedgefield, and for the Durham to Sunderland road. The extent to which these turnpikes improved trade and communications in the region is difficult to assess. Some were clearly of significance for land-sale of coal, and in the lime trade, and more particularly in the lead trade of the North Pennine Orefield. They also helped Cumbrian cloth to get to the Tyne, and hence to the Baltic, more cheaply. But they were not an unmitigated blessing. Moreover, as elsewhere in the country, they only represented a very small fraction of the total road network, and the non-turnpiked roads remained almost universally poor to dreadful.

In general then, the North East shared in the nation's turnpike mania, some nine-hundred miles of turnpikes in the region by 1833, with on average a tollgate every five miles. Some local turnpikes, however, had relatively few tollgates – the Alemouth Turnpike Road (Hexham to Alnmouth, sometimes incorrectly referenced to as the 'Corn Road') for example, was one of the longest turnpikes ever built in the region, some 51½ miles being under the care of its trustees. Its four unevenly spaced tollhouses during the 18th century gave an average of 12.9 miles of turnpike per tollhouse, and with a total aggregate ascent along its route, including a short branch of 4,886 feet and a maximum altitude of 911 feet above sea level, most of its route lying above five-hundred feet above sea level, it was always a difficult route to travel, especially in winter. The state of the turnpikes was widely variable and, as elsewhere in the country, there were constant complaints about them. Moreover, toll revenues to turnpike trusts in England and Wales were to fall by one-third between the years 1837 and 1850, as the 'calamity of the railways' reduced many trusts to near insolvency. They rapidly passed into history from the 1860s.

Waggonway improvements

We can be fairly certain that both the sleepers, or 'dormant timbers' as they were sometimes called, and the rails of the earliest waggonways were of wood, and this remained the case until late in the 18th century. Unfortunately, wood rots quite readily and the rails in particular suffered from wear and rotting. Heavy traffic might mean that wooden rails would only last about a year, so that maintenance of the tracks could be a high running cost for the coalowner. It is perhaps not surprising that a better wearing material, iron, came to be considered for waggonway track, either to protect the most vulnerable sections of wooden rails, or ultimately to replace them completely. The first use of iron on waggonway rails would seem to have been in the form of upper-surface wearing strips, fastened down to vulnerable sections of wooden rail. These were certainly in use before 1765 in the North East, and by the turn of the century, wrought-iron wearing strips appear to have been quite common on local waggonways.

The price of timber rocketed during the period of the Napoleonic Wars, while simultaneously, the price of iron halved, from £22 per ton to £11 per ton, due to a massive expansion of the iron industry and consequent over-production. These market price changes further encouraged the replacement of wood on the waggonways by cast-iron for the rails, and by stone 'sleeper blocks' rather than wooden sleepers; a great advantage of stone sleeper blocks was that they did not deteriorate and since they were not transverse between the rails, the horses' hooves did not come into contact with them. The lower friction presented by cast iron rails meant that horse-work was much reduced per mile of haulage, so that, according to John Buddle, between thirty per cent and one-hundred per cent more work could be obtained from the horses. Naturally then, iron rails became popular on many of the waggonways of the North East. A visitor to Walker Colliery in 1807, recorded:

They are gradually giving up their wood roads, and introducing iron, and they make them piece by piece keeping up the old waggons and running them partly on wood and partly iron.

From about 1800, most new waggonways in the North East, for example the Kenton & Coxlodge waggonway of 1808, used iron rails on stone sleeper blocks and gradually, many older waggonways were thus provided. These were also the materials used on the first steam-hauled railways, the Stockton & Darlington Railway and the Liverpool & Manchester Railway, for example.

However, cast iron is a brittle material, and although a fish-bellied design made the best use of it, the constant jarring of the rails must have caused many failures. Wrought iron, ('malleable iron'), was an obvious alternative, for it was not brittle, and in around 1805, Charles Nixon of Walbottle Colliery laid some narrow malleable iron rails on his waggonway. However, his narrow rails cut grooves into the rims of the waggon wheels and this caused him to abandon the experiment. The next attempt to use wrought-iron rails was made in the unlikely setting of Tindale Fell, Brampton, Cumbria, where 3½ miles of line were laid with broader wrought-iron bars in 1808-12. After having been in use for sixteen years, the rails showed hardly any deterioration when compared with some cast-iron rails on other parts of the same line, many of which had fractured.

Michael Longridge of the Bedlington Ironworks determined to do likewise on a waggonway that he was about to construct, but John Birkinshaw, his agent at the works, believed that he could improve on the Tindale design. Birkinshaw was successful in this attempt, and in 1820 he laid his new waggonway with the improved rails. The new waggonway and its wrought-iron rails were an immediate success, and wrought-iron rails soon had many advocates, not just Longridge and his friend George Stephenson. William James, the original projector of the Liverpool & Manchester Railway, wrote in 1821, in suitably purple prose:

Light has at length shone from the north and I pronounce as my decided opinion that the Malleable Iron Rail Road at Bleddington [sic] Works is by far the best I have ever seen both in respect of its material and its form.

But other changes had been made to the waggonways and their operation that can only be outlined here.

As indicated, the major changes to the waggonways came about as a response to the prevailing economic conditions during the Napoleonic wars. The cost of horses and their fodder soared in that period, which meant that a more efficient use of horses was called for, or even their replacement by something else. In short there was a need to reduce the capital and running costs of the waggonways. This was achieved, in different ways, over several decades in a fairly piecemeal fashion, but the end results were, firstly, a new kind of colliery railway, and secondly, the steam-hauled railway of the 19th century; these three phases of railway development overlapped one another.

A single horse could pull more than one full waggon if the way was level, but the presence of fairly steeply inclined sections of the waggonway effectively prevented the haulage of sets of full waggons, firstly because of difficulties in braking the waggons when going downhill under gravity, and secondly the difficulties experienced by a single horse in returning multiple empty waggons back uphill. Not much could be done about the second of these, except to arrange for spare horses to assist with returning the empties, or to provide an alternative and easier return route. But the first problem could be ameliorated by improving the braking system.

From the beginnings of the waggonways, each waggon had been braked by the man in charge of the waggon sitting upon a brake lever, the 'convoy', which operated on one wheel only. By 1754, some waggons had manual brakes on all four wheels, but it was not until 1795 that a braking system enabled one man and one horse to control two waggons. But the ultimate solution to the braking system was the 'long brake' whereby application of the brake to the rear waggon in a set was automatically applied to the waggons ahead of it. Now haulage of multiple sets was possible, and one horse and one man could handle sets of waggons on the level, or on down gradients with the load. It is not clear just when the use of the long brake first occurred, but the earliest description of it dates from 1834.

We have seen that where the gradient of a waggonway was sufficiently steep, the horse was normally unloosed and allowed to trot behind, the waggonman controlling the descent with the brake(s). It is perhaps surprising then, that it is not until 1784 that we have evidence for a practice in the North East whereby descending full waggons on an incline could be used to simultaneously draw empty waggons back up the incline, that is, a self-acting (gravity) inclined plane; such a system had earlier been used on some canals.

From the 1780s, stationary steam engines were in use as shaft winders in some coal mines, but it would seem that it was not until the Napoleonic war period that such engines were introduced on the waggonways for waggon haulage. Thus, a hauling engine on Birtley Fell in 1808/9, drew waggons from the Team Valley up towards Eighton Banks – the beginnings of the Pelaw Main Railway. Other lines would soon do likewise, and in fact, fixed engines came to be used not only for gradients against the load, but for level sections of line as well.

Replacing the horse

After earlier experiments with a full-size steam carriage in 1797, the Cornishman Richard Trevithick built an experimental locomotive to run on rails at Coalbrookdale, Shropshire, in 1802/3, and then, in 1804, another locomotive that briefly ran on the Pen y Darren tramway at Merthyr Tydfil; these were the first steam locomotives in the world. At the same time he designed a locomotive for Christopher Blackett of Wylam Colliery, intended to be used on the very level, 4½ miles long, Wylam waggonway. This locomotive was built at Gateshead, in John Whinfield's Pipewellgate Works, sometime between October 1804 and May 1805. It was the first steam locomotive ever built in north-east England, and it apparently operated successfully on a temporary track within the works but, for reasons that are unclear, it never left the Gateshead works, remaining there for a while to be used as a fixed engine. Trevithick, the true inventor of the steam locomotive, then disappeared from the scene. He was an adventurous inventor, but neither a visionary nor a businessman. He moved to South America and eventually fell upon hard times. His mantle was assumed by north-eastern engineers.

John Blenkinsop was born at Walker on Tyne in 1782, and in around 1801-2, was appointed viewer to the Brandling's collieries at Middleton, near Leeds, where a level horse-drawn waggonway some four miles long carried coal into Leeds. Apparently aware of Trevithick's successful attempts in building a steam locomotive, he designed a one to work on the Middleton way. However, seemingly in the belief that iron wheels would not provide sufficient friction to drive efficiently on iron rails, he arranged for the locomotive engine to drive a cogged wheel which worked against a toothed rack cast upon one side of the rails. In 1812, his locomotive was put to work on the Middleton railway, and apparently thousands of people came out to see it – it was said to have been 'crowned with success' and to have performed the same work as sixteen horses working for twelve hours. In 1813, the Brandlings decided to use a similar racked railway for their Kenton & Coxlodge line and it opened with some success on 2 September of that year, although one person at the opening celebration, George Stephenson, then enginewright at Killingworth colliery, was reported as being unimpressed. Blenkinsop died at Leeds in 1831, aged forty-eight years, and although the racked railway did not prove to be necessary on level tracks, he had been the first to use a steam locomotive for strictly commercial purposes.

William Hedley, born at Newburn in 1779, was appointed viewer for the Wylam collieries in 1805 where, three years later, the very level Wylam waggonway was converted from wooden rails to cast-iron plate rails. This change of rail surface allowed a single horse to pull two wagons quite easily, but Hedley began to build a steam locomotive for the Wylam Way in 1812. After some experimentation he became convinced that racks and pinions were unnecessary, and that a load could be moved with smooth wheels driving on smooth rails, as indeed Trevithick had previously demonstrated. Hedley then had a locomotive built at the works of Thomas Waters of Gateshead, the successor to John Whinfield. Waters had something of a reputation in the art of boiler and steam-engine making, for if one of his engines seemed disinclined to go, he simply held down the boiler safety valve, declaring that either she, or he, would go! Waters' engine may have worked at Wylam for a short while, but Hedley's next locomotive entered service in 1814-15, and by around 1815 he had three locos in use on the line. Hedley had been helped in his locomotive building by Timothy Hackworth, foreman blacksmith at Wylam, but Hackworth, a staunch Wesleyan local preacher, left the concern, having objected to being asked to work on the Sabbath. He would soon go on to greater fame with the Stockton & Darlington Railway.

The main focus of locomotive development was now to move to Killingworth, but it remained in the hands of another with strong Wylam connections. George Stephenson was born at High Street House, Wylam on 9 June 1781, with the Wylam waggonway running immediately alongside the front door. By 1812, he was engine-wright at Killingworth High Pit, a colliery then owned by proprietors who had clearly watched with interest the developments in steam locomotion by their rivals, the Brandlings at Leeds, and the Blacketts at Wylam. In 1813, Stephenson, who was familiar with Hedley's Wylam locomotives, was asked build a steam locomotive, and his first attempts, *My Lord* and *Blucher*, were running by 1814. Significantly, the track gauge of the Killingworth waggonway was 4ft 8inches, and Stephenson would adopt that gauge for the new railway lines that he was soon to superintend: the present 'standard gauge' throughout most of Europe, and much of the world, derives from the Killingworth Way, an extra half inch being added by 1835 to make the traversing of curves easier for longer rolling stock.

There were other attempts at steam locomotion, both worth mentioning even though they soon passed to where they belonged – obscurity. William Chapman (1749-1832) and his brother Edward patented a steam locomotive, albeit a rather curious one, which hauled itself along rails by powering an endless chain. This device was tried on the Heaton waggonway in October 1813 when, apparently, the device worked, after a fashion, and although another similar engine seems to have been built for a Lambton waggonway in County Durham, it was never a great success. William Brunton (1777-1851) patented his 'horse to go by steam ... capable of being used on a road or railway ... by means of certain levers or legs' in 1813. His steam locomotive was just that! One or more steam cylinders were used to power levers which simulated the ordinary action of walking. A Brunton engine was delivered to Mr Neasham's colliery at Newbottle, Co Durham, in around 1814, where it was put to work on a level section and apparently pulled twelve loaded wagons, but that was more or less that for this most unlikely device.

Enough has been said, to establish the fact that the North East was alive with the idea of replacing horses on the waggonways by some form of inanimate power, and that a small group of people, who probably all knew each other, were alive with inventive ingenuity. The benefits of steam locomotion were soon clear – one horse with one waggon on a waggonway could perhaps haul two tons over twenty miles in one day, whereas one (early) steam loco on a railway could haul up to forty tons over two-hundred miles in one day.

All the technologies were now in place for the second phase of railway development in the North East, still essentially to serve the local coal trade, the begetter of the railways of the 19th century. The way was now paved, not only for the renewal of the older waggonways of the North East, and the creation of new colliery railways in the region, but also for the railway revolution that was about to sweep the kingdom, and indeed, much of the world. For although further changes and improvements were yet to come, stone sleeper blocks and wrought-iron rails, plus the steam locomotive, born of, and developed to serve, the transport of north-eastern coal, were to be the foundation of the modern railway era, and the north east of England continued to provide the main spur to subsequent railway development.

The second phase of railway development in North East England – the Reciprocating Railways

Some new colliery lines were created in the North East to use some or all of the improvements mentioned above. They were sometimes known as 'reciprocating' railways because for every set of full coal waggons travelling via level sections or inclines from the mine to a river staith, a similar set of empty waggons had to be simultaneously worked back towards the pit: these lines also sometimes including horse-worked and locomotive-worked sections. Unlike the horse-drawn waggonways, these more efficient new lines had no need to take the shortest available routes to navigable water, but could head straight towards staiths much closer to the sea, thereby saving river transhipment.

The Hetton Colliery Railway in County Durham was the first of the new railways, and the first line to be engineered by George Stephenson. It opened on 18 November 1822, essentially for the carriage of coal from the Hetton area to the port of Sunderland. It was designed to use steam locomotives where gradients were sufficiently shallow, and inclined planes, both stationary-engine hauled and self-acting, where appropriate. The journey from pit to staith usually took between one and a half to two hours in 1826,

so it was a slow journey, at around 4mph overall. It was slow, partly because of the logistics of reciprocating-railway operation, that is, the need for counter-balancing empty waggons, and the frequent changeovers from one rope to another for different parts of the journey. But, like many a reciprocating railway, it served its purpose – that of carrying coal – extremely well. Most of this line remained open until September 1959, operating for 137 years. Clearly the reciprocating railways were not just a transitionary phase in railway development, for most of them functioned until the collieries that they were built to serve were closed down.

Subsequent reciprocating railway development can only be outlined here. Such lines were mainly, but not exclusively used in the Durham coalfield, where the terrain was more difficult than that of the south Northumberland coalfield, and they included, in Durham, the Pelaw Main Railway (1808/9-1973); the Bowes Railway (with George Stephenson as 'Consulting Engineer' 1826-1974); the Rainton & Seaham Railway (1831-1984); the South Hetton Railway (1833-1984); the Stanhope & Tyne Railway (1834-1985); the Durham & Sunderland Railway, (1836-1991). In Northumberland there were the North Walbottle Railway (around 1815-1968) and the Brunton & Shields Railway (1826-1980).

The Stockton & Darlington Railway

In some ways the famous (because it became famous) Stockton & Darlington Railway fits into this pattern of the reciprocating railways, but because its engineer, George Stephenson, could choose a mainly level route for some twenty miles or so between Shildon and the River Tees at Stockton, partly made possible through the creation of embankments and cuttings, steam locomotives could be used along this section: west of Shildon; engine and self-acting inclines would be used to reach the collieries that the line was intended to serve. Stephenson also recommended wrought-iron rails for the single-track main line, and cast-iron rails for the passing places, set on stone sleeper blocks at the west end of the line, but on oak blocks at the east end. The track gauge would be that with which he was now absolutely familiar – 4ft 8inches. Dandy waggons (see below) were also to be used, but although passengers were hauled by the steam locomotive *Locomotion* in the opening day parade in 1825, that would not happen again until 1833/4, passengers being horse-drawn until then. *Locomotion* had been built at the world's first locomotive-building factory, named after George's son, Robert Stephenson & Co, Forth St., Newcastle, established in 1823.

It was a railway that was much written about partly because it crossed the much-travelled Great North Road at Darlington and was therefore seen by numerous travellers and travel writers. In many respects the Stockton & Darlington railway was an unusual railway, but its precedents lay in the technologies of the colliery lines of the North East, the administrative arrangements of the canals, and to a certain extent, the turnpikes, and in the legal framework of earlier railways that had also been established under Acts of Parliament. It was clearly not the first railway. It was not the first public railway. It was not the first passenger railway. It was not the first railway to use steam locomotives. But it was the first public railway to use steam power, in a combination of stationary engines and locomotives. However, more importantly, it graphically demonstrated, for the first time, the potential of the steam locomotive, and also that easier and cheaper communication actually increased traffic. It was also easily the longest railway in the world at the time of its opening.

To some extent, a growth in horse-hauled passengers on the line caught the Stockton & Darlington Railway unawares, and it was left to the Liverpool & Manchester railway really to demonstrate the great potential for locomotive-hauled passenger transport, albeit between two of the greatest cities of the country, the one a most important port, the other 'Cottonopolis'. In 1824, the provisional committee for the Liverpool & Manchester Railway were so impressed by George Stephenson's locomotives, and by the man himself, that they appointed him Engineer to the Company even before the Stockton & Darlington Railway had opened.

The Dandy Waggon

We have seen that on waggonway runs of appropriate gradient, the horse could trot behind the waggon. Indeed, this was the safest place for the horse to be if the gradient with the load was severe. While this was easy 'work' for the horse, it was demonstrated that if the horse was provided with its own waggon – the 'dandy waggon', a simple four-wheeled bogie – for such descents, then even though the horse had to pull the empty coal waggon and dandy waggon back uphill, the overall workload on the horse was considerably reduced. George Stephenson claimed to have invented the dandy waggon system for the Stockton & Darlington Railway in 1826, and certainly it appears to have been yet another North Eastern development. The Dandy was clearly popular with the horses. One dandy waggon driver, on being asked whether the horse liked the Dandy, observed that 'You would hardly believe it, but ... one day I had not the [Dandy], and the horse was trying to get into a chaldron waggon'. In fact getting on and off the Dandy became mere routine for the horses, for example, in getting off while the waggon was still in motion.

The third phase of railway development – The Steam-hauled Railways.

There were to be many difficulties before the line opened between Liverpool and Manchester in 1830, but the success of the line for the haulage both of freight and passengers led to a scramble for more such railways. Consequently, few areas of the country would remain unaffected by the railway mania that followed, but in the North East a new railway network was superimposed on the earlier waggonways and reciprocating railways, the net result being that the region has probably the most complex rail archaeology and geography in the world. Moreover, the technical, economic and social success of the early steam-hauled railways, and therefore of the railway revolution of the 19th century, was rooted in the ideas, experiences and skills of people who had been involved in improvements to coal carriage in North East England.

The North East's first true railway, in the modern sense, was the pioneering Newcastle & Carlisle Railway. When it was fully open by 1838, it was the first railway across England and, at nearly sixty-five miles, the longest railway in the world at the time of its building. It was the first important line to use standard gauge throughout. It was also the first line to provide passenger facilities at intermediate stations, and the first line to use the once-traditional railway tickets from around 1837.

The York, Newcastle & Berwick Railway of 1849 put the north east region into direct rail communication with the rest of the UK system and gave some outstanding railway monuments to the region, firstly in Robert Stephenson's High Level and Royal Border rail bridges, two of the finest in the country, and secondly Dobson's Newcastle Central Station, which involved new and significant strides in train shed roof design. Other rail routes such as the Border Counties of 1862, the South Durham & Lancashire Union of 1863, the Tees Valley of 1868, the Wear Valley of 1847-1895, and the Cornhill Branch of 1887, plus a host of branches and minor routes, gave the region a good railway system, almost all of which had come under the North Eastern Railway company by 1874.

The nation's turnpikes now suffered 'the calamity of the railways', as more and more people were drawn to rail travel. Even the reciprocating railways of the North East turned to the carriage of passengers as well as coal. Amazingly, it may seem to us now, even such cumbersome means of passenger transport, on lines designed primarily to carry coal, had their appeal for passengers, so much so that such lines were actually able to build up passenger revenues. For example, a specially constructed coach on the Rainton & Seaham railway brought people from the Raintons to shop at Seaham Harbour – on Saturdays only. Dr A. B. Granville, travelling by rail in the area in 1840-41, noted:

If the tourist, on his way to Hartlepool, departs direct from Sunderland, many are the modes and changes which he will witness in the manner of being forwarded to his destination. The manner is a tedious though an extremely cheap one, and as the levels of ground vary, so do the means employed to travel over them. Thus, from the sea village of Ryhope, three miles from the first station out of Sunderland, the traveller will be dragged up an elevated plane, by stationary engines working an endless rope ... and in that manner will he reach Haswell. Of these stationary engines there is one at every three miles; but even that number would not have been sufficient for the intended purpose, had not the ascending ground been rendered less steep, by excavations made ... to a considerable depth.

At Haswell the moving power is again changed, and a single horse, put in front of the whole train, is found to be sufficient to draw the immense loads ... along a single rail. This being upon a gentle inclined plane, the animal finds it no difficult task to proceed at the rate of from eight to ten miles an hour, with all that tremendous tail behind him.

Vision had been required to predict that the railway, in the modern sense of that word, a locomotive-hauled railway system for both freight and passengers, could be a development of revolutionary importance. Not many had that dream as they toiled in the coalfields of the North East, but George Stephenson was an exception. As he informed his Methodist friend, Thomas Summerside, with extraordinary prescience, 'I will send the locomotive as the great missionary over the world', but it is doubtful that even Stephenson foresaw a railway across the Atacama Desert in Chile. Vision alone would not have been sufficient to ensure the development of railways, for technical expertise, political and business acumen, and the prospect of financial profit, were, at the time, also important. However, the progress of railways in the early 19th century, in the United Kingdom, in Europe, in America, etc., owed much to the skills and vision that largely emanated from north-east England, and it was to be a development of immense influence in the subsequent history of the world.

Stafford M. Linsley

A locomotive at Redheugh Station on the Newcastle to Carlisle line, 1838.

Ports and harbours

It hardly needs pointing out that ports and harbours, whether natural or artificial, were crucial to the North East's industrial economy, so dependent was it on the export of coal, both coastwise and foreign, and on a variety of imports. There were some spirited harbour developments in north-east England before the 19th century, but some of those early creations were to falter in the 18th and 19th centuries, and pass into history. Cullercoats Harbour, for example, constructed in 1677 for the shipment of coal and later of salt, had effectively failed by 1724 after the closure of Whitley Colliery; such a small harbour so near to the Tyne was unlikely to survive for long under any circumstances. A few miles to the north the Delavals developed Seaton Sluice and Hartley Harbour from the 17th century onwards for the export of coal, glass, salt and copperas. The little harbour that they created, with its 1760 cut through a sandstone outcrop, illustrates the combination of entrepreneurial flair and technological confidence that was to catalyse much of the North East's industrial development, but it had ceased trading by 1872.

Other river and port improvements accompanied the growing north-eastern coal trade. But if that trade was to take full advantage of the development of, and improvements to railways and 19th century advances in steam shipping, big changes would be needed to the region's ports and harbours, particularly in reducing vessel turn-round times. Some harbour authorities reacted to these changes with alacrity, while others dithered.

The reciprocating railways were essentially feeders for water-borne coal traffic, and since most of them could efficiently reach navigable water where tidal variations were at their maximum, new types of adjustable chutes and coal drops were needed at the coal staiths to replace traditional barrow-and-plank loading and fixed chutes; the latter would have resulted in excessive coal breakage where tidal variations were great. In 1812 'coal drops' were built at Wallsend; they could lower loaded coal waggons directly to the holds of collier brigs, using a platform that was suspended at the end of a huge pivoted and counter-balanced arm. These drops, subsequently built elsewhere on the Tyne, the Wear and the Tees, at down-river locations, effectively dented much of the keelmen's domain. But still by 1860, one-third of the Tyne's coal traffic was carried on keels, particularly above Newcastle's 18th century stone arch bridge where sea-going colliers could never go. The Wear fared somewhat better and was virtually independent of keels by 1860.

River Wear commissioners were appointed in 1716, almost 150 years before the Tyne had similar governance, and although 18th century proposals to extend navigation to the City of Durham were unsuccessful, considerable improvements were made at the mouth of the Wear under the commissioners. As with most north eastern ports, the Wear was to see considerable change in the 19th century. The North Dock for the Wearmouth Dock Co was opened in 1837, and the north pier was extended, resulting in one of the most popular engineering events in Victorian Britain, 'The Lighthouse which moved'. A south dock, called the Hudson Dock, was opened in 1850, and was later extended, particularly by the creation of the Hendon Dock

Opposite, clockwise from top left: 1) *Shoring up the embankment along the quay, thought to be North Shields, c. 1900.* 2) *Tynemouth's North Pier is damaged during a storm in 1897.* 3) *Cullercoats Bay, c. 1900.*

SALT
WATER BATHS.

in 1868. The outer North Pier, constructed 1885-1903 and 2,880 feet long, is still perhaps the longest breakwater in England.

The River Tees had been little improved in the 18th century, and indeed the stone arch bridge built at Stockton in 1769 gradually fossilised the inland port of Yarm, lying seventeen miles from the river's mouth, while at the same time accentuating Stockton's role as a port seven and half miles downriver from Yarm. Some river improvements were made to reduce the sailing distance from Stockton to the sea, notably the Mandale Cut of 1810 and the Portrack Cut 21 years later. But it was only after the opening of the Stockton & Darlington Railway that the Tees became an important coal-exporting river, although Stockton, where staiths had been built in 1826, was gradually overtaken by the creation of the town of Middlesbrough at the 1830/31 downriver terminus of an extension to the Stockton & Darlington Railway – the first town to owe its existence to a railway. Middlesbrough Dock was opened in 1842.

In part, these developments on the Tees had been prompted by advances elsewhere. The coal-shipping harbour at Seaham had opened in 1831, while at Hartlepool, dramatic port expansion followed the opening up of Durham's 'concealed coalfield', initially with the creation of a dock in 1835; by 1841 the Hartlepool Railway was carrying more coal than any other line in the North East – no less than twenty-seven per cent of all the coal shipped from the region. This was followed by the creation of West Hartlepool with extensive dock building between 1847 and 1852; by 1893, two-hundred acres of dock, harbour and basin were in use for coal exports, but considerable quantities of grain, eggs and general goods were also imported. The Hartlepools also developed an extensive timber trade, while the chalky ballast on returning colliers formed the basis of an important Portland cement industry. Hartlepool's success had

probably retarded developments on the Tees although the rivalry between Stockton and Middlesbrough had also hindered overall improvement.

At the northern end of the region the ancient port of Berwick, with Tweedmouth and Spittal, had long lost much of its former importance as a major port for Scotland; it could no longer be described, as it was in 1296, as 'a city so prosperous and of such trade that it might justly be called another Alexandria, whose riches were the sea and the waters its walls'; it was said, at that period, that the annual value of its Customs was about £2,200, while that of the whole of the English ports was only £8,000. Even so, the port retained an established coasting trade with London, and it also reflected the nationwide move towards improvement with its new Tweed Dock, built in the 1860s. Elsewhere in the region, port and harbour developments were evident at Blyth from the 1880s when, under its commissioners and the North Eastern Railway, developments came fast and furious. Annual coal shipments from Blyth had reached one million tons by 1887; the expansion of the Ashington coalfield, and a pricing policy that made shipment from Blyth cheaper than from the Tyne, all contributed to this late-in-the-day success story. Less dramatic, but nonetheless significant, was the progress at Amble harbour during the 19th century.

Meanwhile, to the south, the Tyne, finally freed in 1851 from the stultifying control of the Corporation of Newcastle and placed under the care of commissioners, was subjected to a belated but vigorous programme of improvement. Pier building began in 1855, the Northumberland Dock at Howden, built to serve coal-carrying railways from several collieries in Northumberland, was constructed in 1857, while the fifty acre Tyne Dock at South Shields was built by the North Eastern Railway in 1859 (and rebuilt in 1890). These were the first substantial improvements ever made to the Tyne;

at its zenith, in 1913, some seven million tons of coal and coke were shipped from Tyne Dock's four staiths. The replacement of Newcastle's 18th century stone arch bridge by Armstrong's hydraulic swing bridge of 1876 would open up the river 'above bridge' to direct coal shipments once upriver dredging had been completed. Moreover, navigation above bridge also encouraged the upriver establishment of flour mills and hide works etc, and the expansion of engineering and other industrial developments on that part of the river. The Albert Edward Dock, designed for coal exports and general cargo imports, was created at North Shields by the Tyne Improvement Commission in the 1880s; it could take larger vessels than the Northumberland Dock. By 1887, the river had been sufficiently dredged above bridge to enable the Armstrong Works at Elswick to commence shipbuilding, the North Eastern Railway to create Dunston Staiths in 1893, and the Consett Iron Works to build the Derwenthaugh staiths in 1900.

Although the coal trade provided the main impetus to port and harbour developments in North East England, and remained its mainstay until well into the 20th century, most north eastern ports continued to operate a varied trade. Thus, in common with the general nineteenth-century improvements to the country's ports and harbours, most of the North East region's ports were provided with permanent deep-water docks, improved cargo handling facilities, quays, piers, timber yards, warehouses, granaries, lighthouses, lifeboats, dock offices, etc.

The most remarkable of the region's nineteenth-century ports was, in some ways, the artificial Seaham Harbour, created for the Londonderry family although conceived by an earlier owner of the Seaham estate. Difficulties in shipping coal at Sunderland were the spur to activity at Seaham, yet the harbour plan, which included a planned township to John Dobson's design, was criticised as being 'visionary and absurd'. Not to be put off, however, John Buddle, a Londonderry agent, was even persuaded that Seaham might also become a popular bathing place:

Why may it not become the Weymouth of the North? ... We must have a small steam engine to take the ballast out of the ships [and] with this same engine I could, at a small expence, with small ... pipes throw either hot or cold sea water into every lodging or dressing room in the Hotel or into every private or lodging house in the town. Either plunging or shower baths might be used in every house without giving the inhabitants any trouble whatever except the turning of a cock.

The harbour was completed in 1831 but of Dobson's plan only one terrace of houses was built.

Far from being absurdly visionary, the harbour was already inadequate for the increased coal outputs from nearby collieries by 1853. Consequently, the private Londonderry Seaham & Sunderland Railway was built to link Seaham with the newly opened Hudson Dock at Sunderland. The harbour at Seaham was eventually extended, with a new and impressive array of coal spouts, and although they have now gone, and Seaham no longer exports much if any coal, it still demonstrates in microcosm the interaction between the coal trade and port development in the region during the nineteenth century. In addition it is a physical manifestation of early nineteenth-century entrepreneurial vision rendered myopic by the realities of the Industrial Revolution in full flight.

Stafford M. Linsley

The Ouseburn glasshouses

The first purpose-built glassworks in Britain to use coal as a fuel rather than wood, opened on Tyneside in 1617 near the Ouseburn at East Ballast Hills. The area became known locally as The Glasshouses.

Prior to that date forests and woodlands had been dwindling at an alarming rate due to the relentless felling of trees for some of the emerging industries such as shipbuilding and iron manufacturing, together with the construction of new houses for a rising population. Another reason for the timber shortage was that Huguenot glassmakers settling in England during the 1560s following their persecution in France, were being encouraged by the issue of patents to revive their craft, which had become almost extinct in England.

In earlier times, glass manufacture in the United Kingdom had been insignificant with much window glass and nearly all other glassware being imported from the continent where the quality was usually better. Glass was expensive to make and most Britons would have used wood, leather, stoneware or pewter for everyday articles. To cover window openings, wooden shutters (perforated with small holes) rags or oiled canvas were the norm. Homes of the wealthy were seldom completely glazed and at Alnwick Castle glass windows were removed for safekeeping during the absences of the Earls of Northumberland because of high replacement costs in the 16th century.

Continuing shortages of timber began to result in higher costs and, despite various proposals to protect trees that included moving the glass industry to Ireland and even to America, matters came to a head in 1615 when an Act of Parliament banned the use of wood as a fuel for glassmaking.

Around this time there was a continuing shortage of window glass in London and southern England and in an attempt to solve this problem, a Royal monopoly was granted to Sir Robert Mansell, a forty-five year-old naval officer, for its manufacture somewhere in the UK by the use of coal as an alternative fuel to wood. Mansell was not a technologist but was wealthy and did have a strong decisive personality, as evidenced by his command of a royal warship at a naval encounter and his subsequent knighthood in 1596. Most importantly, Mansell was also considered to possess a 'business brain'.

Royal monopolies were regarded as an inexpensive way to reward deserving servants of the Crown for past services as well as providing revenue for the monarch. Mansell had been obliged by the terms of his monopoly to pay the Crown £1,000 annually 'out of all the profits of the patent'. It seems however this liability was never met, probably because of the enormity of Mansell's development costs – around £28,000 (over three million pounds in today's values) incurred while searching Britain for the ideal location as well as finally setting up the glasshouses near the Ouseburn. Monopolies were also regarded as a way of stimulating trade.

Tyneside possessed major advantages that other areas lacked. First of all there was an abundance of cheap, otherwise unsaleable, coal at a time when the region was the largest coal producing centre in the world. Secondly the three-acre site chosen bordered the Tyne and was therefore ideal for access when few suitable roads existed. Thirdly, raw materials such as sand and flint could be obtained cheaply as ballast from colliers returning to the Tyne for more coal. Finally the North Sea, the gateway to London and the south, was only a few miles away so the cost of transporting glass was lower than it would have been if the glassworks had been located in Nottinghamshire for example.

Apart from being the principal manufacturer of window glass in 17th century England, Mansell also produced glassware not previously made in Britain, such as spectacles and 'crystal plates for looking glasses'. Other products included bottles and tumblers, which were considered preferable to leather or pewter drinking vessels. Most of the output was for export. Destinations included London and the rest of Britain—very little was for the local market.

Thomas Percival invented the coal-fired kiln for glassmaking in 1611, but it was Mansell who pioneered its development by installing larger and more efficient furnaces 'to transform an unstable and scattered art into a genuine industry'. Regarded locally as the 'Father of Newcastle glassmaking', Mansell also controlled the national glass industry for over twenty years until monopolies were abolished by Parliament at the outbreak of the English Civil War around 1642. Towards the end of his career, Mansell claimed that four thousand people nationwide, including the dependants of workers, were supported by his glass industry.

Mansell died in 1652 aged eighty-two and gradually the Ballast Hills business known as The Glasshouses was taken over by Huguenot families that included the Henzells, Tyzacks and Tytorys who made further improvements to the glassworks. In 1736, it was recorded that there were seven glasshouses between the Glasshouse Packhorse Bridge, over the Ouseburn, and the short distance to St Peter's.

The peak of Tyneside glassmaking occurred in the early 1800s when thirty-one glasshouses existed in the area producing forty per cent of English glass. More glass was produced on Tyneside than in France and the product was now ranked locally next in importance to coal.

By 1900, the Ouseburn glasshouses had closed and although part of the area is now occupied by light industry and commercial businesses, the remaining land awaits development. Nothing remains of the glasshouses though names such as Glasshouse Bridge, Glasshouse Street and Bottlehouse Street recall memories of a once significant industry.

The Close glasshouses

In 1684, three brothers called Dagnia arrived on Tyneside from the Forest of Dean area of Gloucestershire and eventually opened four glasshouses in the Close, outside Newcastle's Town Wall. The Dagnias were probably of Italian descent and may well have heard of the Huguenots' success at the Ouseburn and decided 'we must go to Newcastle' where there was excellent river access near the mouth of the Skinnerburn.

One of the glasshouses made window glass and another made bottles, where in 1691 'great quantities of glass bottles were sent beyond seas or coastwise'. Six years later Onesiphorus Dagnia was fined £200 plus costs for fraudulently concealing over 2,679 dozens of glass bottles to avoid a twenty per cent glass tax.

Nothing is known about one of the two remaining glasshouses, but the other business was the first flint glasshouse on the Tyne that specialised in vessels for domestic use. Wine glasses that glistened were in great demand by the merchant class throughout the country and were considered more desirable than pewter tankards for drinking. The Newcastle Light Baluster drinking glass evolved at this glasshouse in around 1730. It had a long stem that resembled a baluster or small pillar supporting a stair handrail in domestic architecture.

A fashion for coloured enamel decoration on drinking glasses from around 1761 encouraged William Beilby and his sister Mary to work for around fifteen years as freelance glass decorators at their workshop near St Nicholas Cathedral. The decorated glasses were fired at the Close glasshouse in kilns adapted for that purpose by William Beilby, who was probably the first Englishman to do this. Newcastle Light Baluster glasses, particularly those engraved by the Beilbys, are now valuable collectors' items and some examples are displayed in local museums and art galleries.

The Dagnia family continued to own the glassworks until 1775 when John Cookson and Company acquired the business. By the mid-19th century these glasshouses had closed. At present the Copthorne Hotel more than covers one site while another location has been landscaped beneath the Queen Elizabeth II Metro Bridge.

South Shields glasshouses

There are a number of theories about the beginning of glassmaking at South Shields, but none of them can be proved. It is likely that it started in the mid to late 1600s following Newcastle's loss of its glass manufacturing monopoly after the English Civil War. There is no documentary evidence to prove which of two glassmaking families was the first to set up in business in the town. One source states that Isaac Cookson's works were in operation by 1704, while another claims that Onesiphorus Dagnia built the first glasshouse in around 1707 for his son John, who had settled at South Shields before 1704.

The earliest written record dates to 1737, when both families, who were already glassmakers in Newcastle, sought to obtain or renew separate leases for glasshouses at South Shields. During the following year John Cookson (son of Isaac) entered into a partnership agreement with another glassmaker to make crown glass and become 'one of the two best window glassmaking firms in England'

though the actual site in South Shields is unclear. In 1756 John Cookson took over the Dagnia glasshouses, as a result of their financial problems, and the Cookson family continued to dominate glassmaking at South Shields for the next ninety years.

By 1827, there were eight large glassmaking works in South Shields making mainly crown window glass and employing a large number of workers in 'one of the greatest glassmaking centres in the country'. Most of these South Shields glasshouses had a Cookson connection.

In the early 1830s 'cast' sheet glass, recently invented on the continent, was beginning to supersede 'blown' crown glass because larger panes of glass could now be made without the awkward central knob or bull's-eye. In order to obtain details of its production method, a foreman at Cookson's volunteered to work as a labourer in a French glasshouse and remain until he fully understood how to build the necessary new type of furnace and then recruit some expert French glassworkers to work at South Shields. Following a successful mission, production of the new product began in 1837.

The Cookson family sold their glass manufacturing business in 1845 to move into the chemical industry and their factory manager R.W. Swinburne became a partner in the new 'Plate Glass Works' along with some high-profile names such as George Stephenson (railway pioneer), George Hudson (railway speculator and MP) and Nicholas Wood (mining engineer). A few years later the South Shields works at the Mill Dam site was adapted to manufacture 'rolled cast plate glass' recently patented by the Sunderland glass maker James Hartley and these two firms shared the enormous order to glaze the Crystal Palace in London in preparation for the Great Exhibition of 1851.

Another reorganisation occurred in 1868 when The Tyne Plate Glass Company was formed. It was eventually headed by Sir C.M. Palmer, the well-known local shipbuilder, on an enlarged seven acre site where around six-hundred workers were employed. Later, as a result of the company's insolvency, glass production at the Mill Dam site ceased in 1891 and for many years the area was occupied by the Harton Coal Company. This location is now landscaped as a recreation park known as Harton Quays, which includes the truncated remains of a brick chimney dated 1865, the sole survivor of the once substantial glassworks.

By 1903 only one glasshouse remained operational at South Shields and that was Edward Moore's pressed glassworks at West Holborn, which continued production for a further two decades.

The Lemington Glassworks

The Northumberland Glass Company was formed in 1791 by six wealthy local businessmen to manufacture crown window glass at Lemington, a short distance west of Newcastle. Eventually the company was considered 'the most complete glass manufactory in England'. These businessmen had previously tried to locate a suitable riverside site in Newcastle but were frustrated because of 'ungenerous opposition'. They sought the help of the Duke of Northumberland who leased them vacant land at Lemington and then named the company after him. Unusually at this period, the factory opened with a complete set of buildings, including four large glasshouses (cones), mainly due to the wealth of the business partners.

About thirty men would have been employed in each cone, working around a central area of heated pots of molten glass. The lofty cones were designed not only to draw air through underground flues to raise the temperature in the kilns but also to enable unpleasant fumes to be dispersed more effectively.

The demand for window glass increased and the business prospered. The company was regarded as a generous employer because it provided 'good wages, free housing and firing (coal) for all employees'. However in 1845, following the abolition of the duty on manufactured glass, the glass trade faced increased competition and lower selling prices resulting in the industry falling into depression. Another problem for the company in the late 1840s was that blown crown glass was being superseded by cast sheet glass, which was cheaper to make and produced larger and better quality panes of glass.

In 1852 the Northumberland Glass Company was put up for sale and then a variety of owners continued to manufacture glass in declining quantities. In 1906 the General Electric Company purchased the site and began to make light bulbs and glass tubes with a workforce of up to three hundred. Further developments followed when associated companies adapted the works to produce TV tubes, components for vacuum flasks and street lighting, which saw the doubling of the payroll to nearly seven hundred.

Following closure of the glassworks in 1997 all the buildings were demolished except the last of the original cone glasshouses. Before being refurbished by English Heritage and Newcastle City Council, the remaining cone was a location in the film adaptation of Catherine Cookson's novel *The Glass Virgin*. Standing 115ft high and with a 69ft base diameter the cone consists of around one and three-quarter million bricks and is one of the most important industrial monuments in the North East. The cone is one of four surviving similar structures in the United Kingdom and is Grade II listed. Today the inside of the cone is used as a business showroom.

Right: Cottages on Cross Row where a group of women do their washing. The Lemington Glass Works dominate the skyline, around 1910.

The Sowerby Ellison Glassworks

The origins of Sowerby's Ellison Glassworks can be traced back to 1807 when Richard Sowerby, from a Cumbrian family, and some others joined two 'established glassmakers' from Stourbridge in the West Midlands to form a new glassmaking enterprise at Gateshead known as The New Stourbridge Glassworks. They leased land alongside the Tyne, at the west end of Pipewellgate, from Cuthbert Ellison, a major landowner on Tyneside and apparently a cousin of the Sowerbys. It is thought it was used as a flint glasshouse.

Some years later, the business came into the possession of John Sowerby, a nephew of Richard, who, in 1846, acquired a nearby bankrupt flint glasshouse in addition to his existing glasshouse, and installed moulding machinery with the aim of producing cheaply priced articles for the mass market. A few years later Sowerby was forced to vacate both glassworks due to the polluted nature of the Pipewellgate area at that time.

In 1852, John Sowerby relocated his business to be near the railway in Gateshead, close to the new High Level Bridge, where he opened a purpose-built glassworks 'all under one roof' on a five-and-a-half acre site. Known as Sowerby's Ellison Glassworks, it had eight ten-pot furnaces, employed around 450 people and was regarded as 'the largest pressed glass factory in the Kingdom'. By 1882, the workforce had reached nearly one thousand and there was continuous round the clock production of drinking glasses, decanters, sugar bowls plus other domestic dishes and plates. In one shift a semi-skilled worker could produce between 1,100 and 1,200 tumblers.

Both John and his son John George were technical innovators and between them they patented several improvements to manufacturing processes, so much so it became increasingly difficult to detect the difference between pressed glass and the more expensive blown glass items. Many of Sowerby's products were noted for their design, decoration and colour which was largely due to John George Sowerby's ability as an artist and illustrator. He had exhibited some of his work at the Royal Academy and various provincial galleries from 1879. Sowerbys made most of the glass for St George's Parish Church in Jesmond, a suburb of Newcastle.

During the 1890s, severe competition both at home and abroad affected the company and, as an experiment, a glassworks was opened in Belgium. It was never successful and closed after several years. By 1907, in Gateshead, more than half of the glass furnaces had been shut down, part of the works had been boarded up and the workforce had dropped to just over three-hundred. Problems continued during and between the World Wars.

Following a takeover in 1957, the works closed in 1972 with the remaining workforce of a hundred and fifty being made redundant. A bingo hall now covers most of the site at East Street. A selection of Sowerby's products can be seen at Gateshead's Shipley Art Gallery and at Newcastle's Laing Art Gallery.

The Tyne Glass Company

The Tyne Glass Company was formed in 1793 by, most unusually, a group of London-based glaziers to take over an existing bottlehouse at Saltmeadows, South Shore, Gateshead and manufacture crown glass. Frequent changes of business partners followed for several years accompanied by bankruptcies, retirements and quarrels over partnership debts and the sharing of profits and losses.

However, in 1810 out of all this turmoil, two London-based glass merchants, previously unconnected with the Saltmeadows business, unexpectedly inherited a share in it from a partner about to retire. The youngest of this pair of glass merchants was twenty-year-old Charles Attwood, the son of a very wealthy Shropshire ironmaster and banker, who saw a future in glass manufacturing and was able to buy out, after a few years, the other Saltmeadows partners largely through his connection with the Attwood family bank.

In 1817, the ambitious Attwood patented the use of pure manufactured soda and lime as a replacement for kelp (seaweed), which had been the traditional alkali used in the manufacture of glass. The patent proved to be a significant milestone in the advance of industrial chemistry that improved the quality and colour of crown glass by making it more transparent and free from blemishes. Attwood's glasshouse became highly profitable and his crown glass circular discs measured up to five feet in diameter, which meant larger squares of superior quality glass could be obtained from each of them.

Following the end of the fourteen year patent in 1831, the Saltmeadows glasshouse lost its pre-eminence to competitors in the crown glass industry such as Cookson's of South Shields and R.L. Chance of Birmingham. At the same time Attwood, a powerful orator, became involved in local politics. In 1840, the Saltmeadows works were sold to Christian Allhusen, the German chemical manufacturer whose works eventually covered 137 acres of the South Shore area, now the site of the East Gateshead Riverside Park and the International Stadium.

Charles Attwood, having tired of the glass industry, founded the Weardale Iron and Coal Company at Tow Law in County Durham in 1846. There he opened five blast furnaces near local supplies of iron ore, limestone and coal and saw the hamlet's population rise from a mere thirty to around five thousand.

Alan Morgan

Large wooden crates are used to transport goods from Lemington Glass Works to the nearby railway siding.

Stone

According to Gray in his *Chorographia* (1649), 'A Scot a Rat and a New Castle Grindstone, you may find all the World over', reason enough why grindstones became almost as symbolic of the Tyne's trades as coal. But most of the grindstones, and certainly the best grindstones, came not from Newcastle as such, but from the Gateshead area. John Hodgson noted in his *Picture of Newcastle* (1812), that grindstones were almost exclusively procured around Windy Nook, Gateshead Fell, and Eighton Banks/Springwell, and it is more than likely that this had always been the case. There were said to be twenty-three quarries in Heworth Township alone in 1832, but during the 19th century, some grindstone quarries were opened to the north of Newcastle, notably at Kenton, Burradon and Wideopen; while these quarries clearly contributed to the Tyne's export of grindstones, the Gateshead quarries remained the major suppliers of 'Newcastle Grindstones'.

What marked out the sandstone from which these grindstones were procured, was its hardness and tenacity, derived from its close-grained structure, and the sharpness of its grit. Generally, the harder a stone, the harder it is to quarry, and the more expensive it is to purchase, but clearly many throughout the world deemed it worth paying for the quality inherent in the 'Newcastle Grindstone'. This sandstone was also used for pulpstones, (large quantities of these being exported to the US for its wood-pulp mills, for example), rubstones, whetstones, and firestones, and also as a building stone, for example for the Shipley Art Gallery in Gateshead, the Armstrong College, Crows Nest pub and Grand Hotel in Newcastle.

In the early part of the 20th century an average of one-hundred and fifty tons of grindstones were said to have left the Tyne every week, the largest of which were ninety-six inches in diameter by fifteen inches in thickness, and destined for Russia which at that time was one of the world's major importers of grindstones. In 1916, in addition to home consumption, some 15,000 tons of grindstones were annually exported from the Tyne to destinations in many parts of the world, but principally to Russia, Norway, Sweden, Denmark, Holland, Belgium, France, Italy, Japan, the USA, Australia, New Zealand, Canada, India and South Africa.

But by the 1950s, the Heworth quarries were surrounded by housing, some having been abandoned and dangerously water-filled. Consequently, in around 1970, Felling Urban District Council declined to renew the lease on the last working quarry in the area, Heworth Burn quarry, although there was said to be enough stone there for another fifty years of operation. All the quarries were subsequently filled in, one site becoming a cricket field.

One of the leading firms in grindstone manufacture was Richard Kell & Company, formed 1784 when that concern acquired land in the Windy Nook and Springwell areas: the business remained in the family until 1942. Their exports from quarries at Windy Nook, Eighton Banks and 'Leamhead-on-Tyne' included grindstones and pulpstones to the Continent, India, the United States, Canada, and Australia. In 1942, the firm was incorporated into Jas. H. Harrison Ltd., formed in 1927. Harrison's also came to specialise in grindstones for whaling factory ships throughout the world. Moreover, a Harrison publicity booklet of c.1970, states that 'For the past one-hundred years grindstones have been supplied to the whole of the Knife and File industry in Sheffield, England'.

Another important local concern was Robson & Co. of Newcastle, 'Grindstone and Millstone Manufacturers [and]

Right top: Grindstones hewn from the rock at Kenton Quarry, 1920s. Right bottom: Rough stone blocks are transformed to grindstones at Windy Nook Quarry, Gateshead.

Quarry Owners'. This business, like so many others of the period, had been handed down from father to son with unbroken regularity, probably from the late 18th century. The firm would come to occupy quarries at Wideopen, Brunton, Burradon, and Clifton Crag (Morpeth), supplying stones used for grinding iron and steel plates and castings used in the construction of locomotives and other engineering work, also stones for cutlery and file-grinding, curriers' rubstones, etc. Robsons also supplied industrial glass furnaces using a refractory 'firestone' from their Wideopen Quarry, as well as millstones and building stone. A few extracts from one of their letter books indicates the range of their sales:

11 November 1889, to Messrs James Lundgren & Co, Goteberg. Four further grindstones, 48 x 7, in addition to the three already ordered; for grinding tools used by engineers.

12 March 1890, to Mr J Wejimont, Anvers [Antwerp, Belgium]. I send you two specimens for pulp stones, one is similar to that previously sent, which I think you will find much harder than the other & quite hard enough for the purpose.

24 May 1890, to Messrs Vickers, Sons & Co, Sheffield. Yours of 23rd to hand, will endeavour to forward part of grindstones on order next week. I am sorry one of the stones sent has turned out a waster, I will replace it. Is the crack a natural defect in the stone, or due to carriage?

21 July 1890, to Messrs J Vartanian & Co, Constantinople. I know that grindstones are sold cheaper than mine, but they are not of the same quality.

10 April 1891, to Mr John Ferguson, Contractor, St. Marys Place, Newcastle on Tyne. We offer to supply you with the stone you require for the New Building at corner of Blackett Street & Pilgrim Street, Newcastle on Tyne, from the best and soundest post of Brunton Quarry.

A number of indigenous millstone sources were worked throughout North East England, and even if they were less favoured than the imported Peak Greys from Derbyshire, the Cullin Blues from Germany, and the French Burrstones from the Paris Basin, there had clearly been a long-standing demand for them. Thus, an advertisement in the *Newcastle Courant* of 18 March 1731/2 has:

Apply to Joseph Liddell, Merchant, Newcastle or Mr Jonathon Maughan of Wolsingham who will furnish any that hath occasion with very good Mill-Stones at Moderate Prices either at the Millstone Quarries at Wascrow [Waskerley] Park or Collier Law.

Another producer of locally-sourced millstones was Brockholm Quarry, a few miles south of Haltwhistle, from where 122 millstones were supplied to some forty destinations between 1842 and 1847, mainly in northern England and southern Scotland.

Imported Burr stones, which came to be regarded as the best for wheat milling, and available in Newcastle by 1800, were not monolithic, but around fifteen pieces of Burrstone would be assembled into a single millstone by urban millwrights and millstone manufacturers, who often also dealt in grindstones. Locally these included Robert Patterson of Newcastle, Robert Atkinson of Felling Square and Skinnerburn, (whose stones were said to be 'Celebrated for their Uniform and Keen Rasping Qualities'), and R. Kell of Gateshead. At the 1929 Newcastle Exhibition, Patterson exhibited 'Grindstones, Millstones (for Oatmeal and Barley) and Pulpstones etc. all produced and manufactured at our quarries in Northumberland'; one of their Northumberland quarries was at Bearl, near Ovington, where millstones continued to be made until c.1940. However, it would be true to say that millstone manufacture was never as significant as grindstone manufacture in North East England.

Stafford M. Linsley

Public utilities

Public utility industries are a necessary feature of a civilised society, their general purpose being to relieve individuals of any personal concerns and responsibilities for certain services. The public utilities were therefore a fundamental facet of the Industrial Revolution – the unspectacular but absolutely necessary tasks of supplying water, gas, good drains, sewage removal, and eventually electricity. Without such provisions a developed urban civilisation could hardly have existed, yet they were, in the 19th and 20th centuries, a novel feature of 'civilised society' when, for the first time in human history, individuals became dependent upon unseen people, often working many miles away, for 'essential' services.

Water supply

Water supply of is one of our most widespread utilities, and is perhaps somewhat unusual in being devoted solely to a single product. Water supplies have been needed, and sometimes desperately needed, for life, for crops, and for power; they have been, therefore, essential for healthy living and for progress in agriculture and industry.

The population of Great Britain doubled between 1801 and 1851 while industry and urban growth developed at an unprecedented rate, but the political framework was not initially particularly sympathetic to a greater regulation of urban life. Water supply became the most significant of the early public utilities, water for domestic, industrial, street cleaning, and fire-fighting purposes. But it was not generally taken seriously in North East England until after cholera epidemics, which occurred between the 1830s and the 1860s, and the 'sanitary idea' that developed from them in the 1840s and 50s – the realisation that good, clean water and efficient drainage were essential to healthy living. Only then did government take a serious interest in water supply, and Acts of 1847 and 1848 gave increased governmental control, and local authority powers, over the nation's water supplies. Moreover, a new urban pride was being encouraged and, in the provision of water, this galvanised the promotion of public and private water supply companies.

The major problem for water supply engineers and the public companies who employed them, was to anticipate future demands and to engineer their supply schemes accordingly. Some concerns succeeded in doing this very well, the Sunderland & South Shields Water Company, for example, while others, such as the Newcastle & Gateshead Water Company, struggled for much of the 19th century. Overall, progress was slow, but sure.

Early public water supplies in North East England were taken from its rivers, from springs, and from fairly shallow wells. The potential for better and larger supplies lay in additional river abstraction, (although progressive contamination pushed abstraction points further upstream), from the use of more remote high land for surface reservoirs, and from the development of the magnesian limestone aquifer in eastern County Durham. Although several small water concerns were to be formed in the 19th century – the Weardale & Shildon Waterworks Company of 1865, the Consett Waterworks Company of 1860, the North Shields Water Company of 1898 etc. – the region's supplies would come to be dominated by the Newcastle & Gateshead, and the Sunderland & South Shields concerns.

There had been a few late 17th and 18th century attempts to improve water supply to Newcastle and

Gateshead, but it was not until the Whittle Dean Water Company was formed in 1845 that they met with any success. The main aim of the company was to rid the citizens of Gateshead and Newcastle of any dependency on Tyne water by constructing reservoirs at Whittle Dean, some eleven miles west of Newcastle, and piping the surface water into the two towns, with a pumping station near the Tyne to deliver water to the Carr Hill reservoir in Gateshead. However, the demand for water had doubled within two years of the scheme being completed, with the result that the company was forced to revert back to Tyne river abstraction from a pumping station at Elswick. But concurrent attempts to provide water from the Tyne, and to dispose of sewage into the same river, almost inevitably spelled trouble. As an indication of the nature of that problem, Pipewellgate in Gateshead, had 2040 inhabitants in 1842, but only three privies (and presumably very long queues). After further cholera outbreaks in the region in 1850 and 1853, the water company seems to have deemed it prudent, in 1855, to replace their Elswick pumping station with one nearer the Tyne's tidal limit, at Newburn, while at the same time increasing their reservoir capacity at Whittle Dean, and later to build an additional reservoir at East Hallington.

The Whittle Dean Water Company was incorporated as the Newcastle & Gateshead Water Company in 1863, but the new company had just as chequered a start as its predecessors, for although it made some improvements, it continued to need Tyne river water, establishing a new river abstraction station at Wylam in 1874. In fact it was not until the successful completion of the 1894/5 Catcleugh Reservoir, near the headwaters of the river Rede in rural Northumberland that the company got ahead of the game.

The Sunderland & South Shields Water Company, on the other hand, became a shining example of progressive water abstraction and supply. That success was in no small measure due to two factors. Firstly, colliery sinkings to the 'concealed coalfield', which lay beneath the thick magnesian limestone strata of East Durham, had demonstrated very large, predictable, and self-renewing reserves of clean water lying within the magnesian limestone. Secondly, the company was be guided by their consulting engineer, Thomas Hawksley, originally from Nottingham, whose reputation became justly established as the most gifted water supply engineer of his day.

In some respects, Hawksley's job was fairly simple, given the magnesian limestone aquifer at his disposal, and he developed an empirical rule that any new water pumping station should be at least two miles from any other. Consequently, he merely had to persuade the company to look ahead, and be as brave and foresighted as himself. Thus large steam-powered pumping stations were to be established at Humbledon (1850), Fulwell (1855), Cleadon (1862), Ryhope (1868), and Cold Hesledon (1877). At the Sunderland Company's Annual General meeting in 1866 it was noted that Hawksley 'had very great experience, and though his ideas had several times appeared to them [the Directors] to be a little too large, and he seemed to be going a little too fast, they had always found, in the long run that they were right in following [his advice] and making things larger each time.' The company directors also noted at this and other meetings, how well they were doing in comparison with the Newcastle & Gateshead Company.

In fact, both concerns were to move quite strongly into the 20th century, but with a greater emphasis on catchwater reservoirs; after Catcleugh came the Burnhope (1937) and Derwent (1967) reservoirs in County Durham, and Northumbrian Water's Kielder reservoir (1981) in Northumberland, the latter being one of the largest man-made lakes in Europe, and situated in one of Europe's largest man-made forests. Soon all the north-eastern water concerns would come under the umbrella of 'Northumbrian Water'.

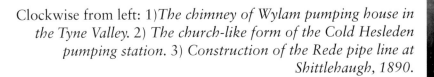

Clockwise from left: 1) *The chimney of Wylam pumping house in the Tyne Valley.* 2) *The church-like form of the Cold Hesleden pumping station.* 3) *Construction of the Rede pipe line at Shittlehaugh, 1890.*

Top left: *Female labourers at Redheugh Gasworks during World War Two.*

Top right: *Blaydon Gas Works. In November 1853 street lighting was introduced to Blaydon, the gas supply being obtained from the works of Messrs. Joseph Cowen & Co., who originally intended the lighting solely for their factory; but at the request of the residents of the area, extended the lighting, to illuminate the town of Blaydon and other neighbouring villages. The gas was made from cannel coal, which gave a very pure gas and a brilliant flame.*

Left: *Forth Banks Power Station, the control dials on the back wall read: Central Station, Quayside B, Empire, Westgate, Quayside A, Clayton Street A, Grainger Street B and Grainger Street A.*

Gas supply

Like other service industries, the gas industry became central to the Industrial Revolution, as it also came to be seen, and is still seen, as an indispensable feature of civilised life.

The idea that gas from coal could be used as an illuminant was first examined in the 17th century, and in 1792, the Scotsman William Murdock carried out larger scale experiments and lit his home in Redruth with coal gas. Meanwhile, Sir Humphrey Davy had ridiculed the idea of illuminating a single building, let alone a town, with gas, as some were suggesting. However, in 1816, 144 Pilgrim Street, Newcastle, the home of Mr Anthony Clapham, was lit by gas, presumably from a small private works and this marked the very beginning of coal-gas lighting in the town; two years later Newcastle's Mosley Street was lit by gas – seemingly the first street in the world to be so lit. (Later the very same street was the first in the kingdom to be lit by electric lighting.) By the mid-19th century almost every large town in the United Kingdom was lit by gas, but this was not always without its problems. On 6 January 1820, a Mrs Slater, smelling gas in her home in Forth Street, Newcastle, sent her daughter to investigate a dark cupboard with a candle, and the resulting explosion wrecked their house and those of her neighbours.

Soon several gas companies were brought into being, the first in Newcastle being 'The Coal Gas Works', which was commenced on Forth Street by the Newcastle Fire Office in 1817, although it is not clear why a fire insurance company should diversify in this way; soon after, there was another works in Manor Place. By 1827 there were 269 public gas lamps within the walls of the town, although only seventy of them were lit on nights when there was a clear full moon. That same year had seen the formation of another gas company, 'The Newcastle Subscription Gas and Light Company', with a works in Sandgate, and after having taken over a small gas company based in Gateshead, with a works in Pipewellgate, the joint concern eventually became known as the Newcastle & Gateshead Gas Company.

But it is apparent that the promoters of these early gasworks were quite unaware of the potential demand for their product, for all were built on extremely constricted sites. Demand for gas was to grow fifteen-fold in the years 1829-1860, and the existing gaswork sites offered no room for expansion. The bullet had to be bitten, and the Newcastle & Gateshead Gas Company therefore commissioned a new works at Elswick, partly to meet the new demands of the Grainger/Dobson development of the town; it opened 1859/60, and both the Manors and Sandgate works were closed down. The company then opened the Redheugh Works in around 1876 at a cost of £100,000, its operational area now covering eighty square miles. It continued to grow, partly by absorbing smaller neighbouring concerns – those at Walker, South Shields and Morpeth for example.

The pattern was rather similar in the major north eastern towns, but a few smaller gas concerns continued into the 20th century, as at Tweedmouth and Hexham. Some coal mines also made gas for distribution to their associated villages, at Cambois and Netherton in Northumberland, for example, and South Hetton and Harraton in County Durham.

It is worth noting that the gas industry was born out of a demand for good, cheap lighting, in the form of fish-tail burners in the early 19th century, and it was not until late in that century that it had any competition in this area – from electricity. Although the gas industry had once been quite vigorous, it had grown conservative, and only after

Lemington Power Station, c.1903.

electricity came along did it rethink its position, towards gas heating, for example, and improved gas lighting through the development of the gas 'mantle' in 1880-90. But all in all, the gas industry steadily improved, and continues to improve, the quality of life for many.

The discovery of substantial reserves of 'natural' gas beneath the North Sea in the 1960s foreshadowed the rapid end of the coal gas industry, and coal gas works were closed down at an unseemly rate. However, we may see locally produced gas again as North Sea gas resources have been depleted at a faster rate than once anticipated. And as there are still large reserves of coal within Britain, it is not inconceivable that local coal gas might yet return in some form or other.

Electricity supply

Investigation of electrical phenomena was well underway from the 18th century, and the beginnings of generation and supply technology developed in the late 19th century, one of the few such developments to receive significant assistance from 'science' and scientists. These developments are of special interest in the North East. As R.A.S. Hennessey put it, in his book *The Electric Revolution*:

Tyneside has many claims to be called the one true source of the electricity industry: here Swan made his discoveries on the incandescent lamp; Parsons perfected his reaction turbine; Charles Merz started 3-phase industrial power and erected the first real central power station with integrated control in Great Britain.

From its beginnings in the last quarter of the 19th century, world demand for electricity has almost doubled every ten years, and it seems not unlikely that this trend will continue, or even accelerate in the future, just as we are running out of fossil fuels. Some saw this coming. In c.1899, W.M. Glover, a Newcastle architect noted:

We are now drawing to the close of the century. On reviewing it we must feel that it is the greatest in the history of this Empire … it is associated with … the power of steam, hydraulics and electricity, the last of which, now only in its infancy, may be regarded as the future propeller, illuminator and chemical agent.

The original purpose of electrical lighting supply was for illumination by arc lamps (Souter Point lighthouse at Whitburn was the first ever lighthouse to be designed with arc lamps in mind) and early lamp patents became a major economic resource for electrical engineering companies. But the north-easterner Joseph Swan demonstrated his prototype of a filament lamp to the Newcastle Chemical Society in 1878 (the world's first practical carbon filament electric lamp) while the American Thomas Edison did something similar about ten months later. Swan's first lamp only lasted a few minutes before excessive current burned it out, but he was soon touring the country with the promise of better electric lighting for domestic purposes, where arc lights were too bright, and sometimes rather dangerous. Swan lit his own home, Underhill, on Kells Lane in Gateshead, with electric incandescent filament lamps, in 1880 – the first in Britain, and probably in the world to be so illuminated. Swan was a friend of W.G. Armstrong, and Cragside, Northumberland became (probably) the second home in Britain to use electric lighting, and also the first in the world to be lit using hydro-electric power. In January 1882, Coxon & Co., drapers of Collingwood Street Newcastle, (or possibly Mawson & Swan's shop in Mosley Street), was the first commercial property anywhere in the world to be lit by Swan lamps.

To capitalise on the great potential of his invention, Swan established the first electric light bulb factory in the world – the Swan Electric Light Company – at Benwell,

Newcastle, in a former tannery. However, the concern was moved to Ponders End in Middlesex in 1886, while Swan himself moved to Kent. This was an early example of a drift of enterprise from north to south in order to make best use of what would inevitably be its major market – London – but perhaps also to minimise breakage of lamps in transit.

A widespread demand for electric lighting now arose quite rapidly, bringing with it additional demands for electric power supplies, and soon every town had its own power station, and sometimes more than one. The major electricity supply companies in the North East were the Newcastle & District Electricity Light Co. ('Disco' – the brain-child of Charles Parsons), and the Newcastle upon Tyne Electricity Supply Co. (Nesco), both formed in 1889. These were followed by the Walker & Wallsend Union Gas Company, with an electricity undertaking in 1901, and the Newcastle upon Tyne Corporation Tramways in the same year. Also established were the County of Durham Electric Power Distribution Co., the Tyneside Power Co and the Cleveland & Durham Electric Power Co. In time, Nesco would absorb all of these concerns.

In common with the gas industry; the early power stations were located as near to urban centres as possible, with little expansion anticipated. In Newcastle, for example, they were located on constricted sites near the city centre, but adjacent to river-water supplies for cooling purposes. Forth Banks Station (Disco 1889/90), for example, was housed in premises on a steeply terraced site by the Tyne, and was the first power station in the world to use steam turbines, built by Charles Parsons. By 1902 Disco had built Close Power Station only a few yards away by the riverside on a site just vacated by Scott & Mountain, the electrical engineers, and then Lemington Power Station in 1903. Nesco, backed by John Theodore Merz (father of Charles Merz), was not originally seen as a rival to Disco for it would operate in different supply areas, and its first

power station was also on a constricted site in Pandon Dene, Newcastle, where it was very soon realised that expansion was necessary; from this small beginning grew a company that would come to supply most of the area to the east of the Pennines from the Tweed to Skipton.

Both Nesco and the Cleveland & Durham Company were able to build up considerable loads by running transmission lines to colliery substations, and by 1911 a number of large collieries were on supply, only a small fraction of them choosing to generate their own power, and then generally only when they had available waste heat from their coke ovens. The most developed of the early colliery systems was undoubtedly that installed by the Harton Coal Company – by 1911 the average daily power demand at Harton Colliery was 1,500 horse power and there was no steam machinery at all at the colliery.

In Newcastle, the first electric trams ran in 1901, operated by the corporation and supplied from their newly built Tramway Power Station at Manors, which also supplied electric lighting to parts of the city; south of the Tyne the County of Durham Electric Power Company had set up Gateshead's electric tramways. Under the impact of tramway competition for passengers, while at the same time helping out Nesco's load building programme, the North Eastern Railway electrified some of its North Tyneside suburban lines; the first electric train passenger service starting in 1904, but replaced by diesel railcars in 1967. Electric traction was also used on the Shildon to Newport Line in County Durham between 1915 and 1934.

The First World War period saw uses for electric power expand dramatically throughout the country, and it should, by then, have been clear that some rationalisation was required, for there existed a plethora of suppliers and systems. London was the most confused district, for by 1917 it had seventy different suppliers, and hence seventy power stations, fifty different types of system, ten different frequencies and twenty different voltages. The North East had not, however, followed the national pattern, and by 1916 the use of electricity per head of its population was from four to ten times greater than that in other districts of the UK. The North East had a relatively uniform and coherent supply, with a reasonably integrated power network.

This situation was largely thanks to people like Charles Merz, whose first major foray into electricity generation and supply was with the Walker & Wallsend Union Gas Company. In 1898, this company sought a Provisional Order to generate and supply electricity, and employed Charles Merz as consulting engineer. Merz designed the Neptune Bank power station at Wallsend on Tyne for the company, aiming to create a power station on a large scale for general supply. It would supply 3-phase AC at 5kv, 40hz, to shipyards, houses, street lighting etc. – Britain's first such supplier of 3-phase 'bulk supply' electricity for industry. To celebrate its opening in 1901, *The Electrician* (21 June 1901) wrote that the undertaking had 'the honour of being the first Statutory Undertaking in the United Kingdom to supply electric power in 'bulk' for motive power purposes in works etc.' It added that 'not merely electric power supply on Tyneside was formally inaugurated last Tuesday, but the era of electric utilisation all over the Kingdom'. No less a person than Lord Kelvin formally opened the new station in 1901, remarking that:

We have seen at work what many have not seen before – a system realised in which a central station generates power by steam engines and delivers electricity to Consumers at distances varying … from a ¼ of a mile to over 3½ miles.

Neptune Bank was thus the first power station in the UK to supply industrial power, as opposed to just electricity for lighting, but it would soon be superceded by Nesco's new power station at Carville, also designed by Merz, and opening in 1904 as a source of supply for the whole of the North East coast, partly by virtue of a cable tunnel constructed under the Tyne. Carville was the first modern central power station with integrated control in Great Britain. Under Merz, Nesco gradually spread its sphere of influence, taking over many smaller companies including Disco (but not the municipal suppliers in Sunderland, Tynemouth and Darlington); the result was that the North East of England had a regional grid before any other area in the country, and Nesco would soon be described in the House of Commons as 'a model which we should like to see the whole of England follow'. In many ways, the rest of the country did just that.

It was not all 'hi-tech' however. At one time Nesco used ferrets to pull string through conduits so that the string could be used to pull cables through. One such ferret failed to emerge from the conduit so they sent a rat in to tempt it out. The ferret promptly ate the rat and jammed itself solid. The conduit had to be dug up to clear the blockage.

Stafford M. Linsley

Chemicals

The insatiable demand for alkali by the huge Tyneside glass trade provided the stimulus for the large-scale development of the chemical industry along the river's banks. In 1791, Frenchman Nicholas Leblanc had invented a process by which alkali (soda) could be made from common salt rather than by laboriously extracting alkali from plant ash (potash). The Leblanc method enabled a variety of chemical-based products to be made on an industrial scale for the first time including soap, bleaching powder and candles.

By the 1860s, Tyneside's twenty-four chemical works produced over half the national output of alkali and during this decade the number of people employed in the industry along the river peaked at over 10,000.

Working in a chemical factory was a hard and dangerous occupation. High temperatures and choking gases were a constant hazard, and unsurprisingly, many of the workmen drank heavily. Public houses were often close to the works, and in at least one case actually inside the premises.

The health of workers suffered, and some lost their teeth because of exposure to chlorine. Bleach-packers, who worked in a chlorine-laden atmosphere, masked their faces in several yards of flannel, kept their nostrils covered and wrapped their trouser legs in brown paper. Goggles were provided, but not always worn. Lime-dressers were exposed to lime dust as well as chlorine so they wore flannel masks and covered their arms and hands with grease to protect against lime burning. Workers were also prone to respiratory problems, such as bronchitis and bronchial catarrh and regularly suffered minor acid burns.

The river's chemical trade was pioneered by the Walker Alkali Works, founded by John Losh, the son of a Cumbrian landowner, and the Earl of Dundonald in 1797. They had previously set up a small alkali business, known as Losh & Company, at Bell's Close on the western side of Newcastle and had experimented with attempts to produce soda from common salt. The partners later moved east to Walker, where a spring of brine (much saltier than sea water) had been discovered in a colliery shaft that was interfering with the output of coal. In order to avoid a crippling salt tax, Dundonald negotiated with the government to add soot and ashes to the salt produced to ensure it could not be used for domestic purposes. This meant that an excise official had to live at the works to make certain that this was done.

Following the move to Walker, the partners were joined by William Losh, a younger brother of John, who had trained in chemistry at Cambridge University. William Losh, who had been a founder of the adjacent Walker Iron Works, eventually became a key figure in both concerns.

In 1802, the partners managed, after considerable difficulties caused by the aftermath of the French Revolution, to obtain the secrets of the Leblanc method and the works became the first factory in England to adopt this process. Despite losing some of its competitive advantage following the repeal of the salt tax in 1823, the business continued to produce soda using the Leblanc method until its closure in the 1870s.

The process was, however damaging to the environment. Unpleasant waste heaps of sulphur deposits were created

Next page, clockwise from top left: 1) *Soda workers at Wallsend, reproduced from 'The Old Tyneside Chemical Trade' W.A. Campbell, 1964. 2) Walker Alkali Works, shown on the 1858 Ordnance Survey map. 3) Felling Chemical Works, c.1833. 4) The turrets of Newcastle Chemical works built to resemble those of the Castle Keep, c.1881.*

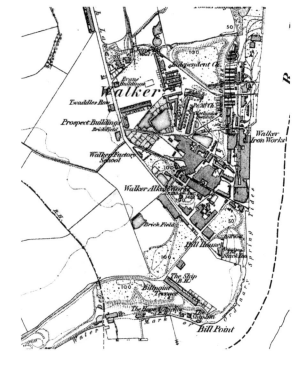

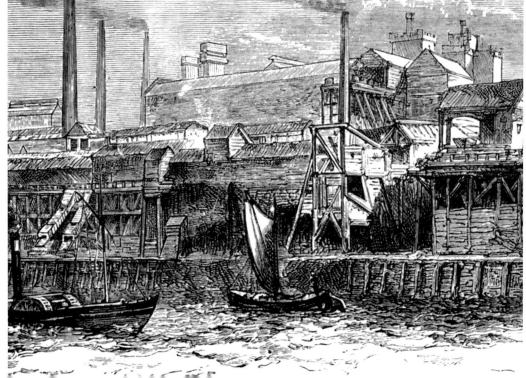

and chlorine gas discharged from the works destroyed vegetation. Tall chimneys did not prevent this nuisance and the Walker area gained a reputation as being unhealthy.

In 1872, a new process for making soda was developed by the Solvay brothers of Belgium and as this needed far less coal than the Leblanc method, it became more convenient to site chemical works near brine deposits rather than coal mines. This led to the decline of the Tyneside industry and to the development of chemical manufacturing on Teesside where huge brine/salt deposits existed. By the 1890s the number of chemical works along the Tyne had plummeted from twenty-four to four and only one remained by the 1920s.

The Walker Alkali works closed during the 1870s and interestingly 'Alkali Farm' appeared nearby on an 1895 Ordnance Survey map of the area. By 1913, the Walker Naval Shipyard had more than covered the site of the former chemical works and today the Walker Riverside Industrial Park occupies the location. Losh Terrace in residential Walker is a reminder of the Losh brothers' important contribution to its chemical and iron industries.

Another chemical firm had been set up by Christian Allhusen, a successful German businessman, at Saltmeadows on the South Shore, Gateshead, in 1840. This concern manufactured soap, alkali, Glauber Salts and Epsom Salts. In 1873, it became the Newcastle Chemical Works Company Ltd., a site which occupied 137 acres.

Sulphuric acid was another of the company's main products, and interestingly, four of its tall acid chambers were topped by turrets and battlements to resemble those of Newcastle's Castle Keep.

Employment peaked in 1889 when 1,200 people worked for the company. The business which had its own railway sidings, riverside wharves and jetties was taken over by the United Alkali Company in 1891 and caustic soda became its main product.

During the 1920s, the business entered a steep decline and in 1926, Imperial Chemical Industries absorbed what was left of the United Alkali Company. The last chimney of the Saltmeadows works was demolished in 1932. Today, the site is covered by East Gateshead Riverside Park and Gateshead International Stadium.

In 1827, Anthony Clapham opened a chemical factory at Friar's Goose and began to manufacture soap. By 1831, soda as well as soap was being produced. Two years later, a 263ft-high chimney, the tallest on the river, was completed at the works. The chimney was intended to disperse noxious gases from the manufacturing processes far above the Tyne's banks.

From 1852 to 1858, the Friar's Goose Chemical Works was operated by a company known as Gray & Crowe. It produced bicarbonate of soda and Epsom Salts as well as alkali. The business collapsed in 1858, but was taken over by the Jarrow Chemical Works, thereby creating the largest firm in the trade on Tyneside, employing 1,400 workers. In 1891, both factories were taken over by the United Alkali Company. The Friar's Goose works closed before the First World War and the site today is part of East Gateshead Riverside Park.

The Felling Shore Chemical Works was opened in 1833, on a site to the west of Stoneygate Lane and near the river, by John Lee, Hugh Lee Pattinson and George Burnett. Its main products were sulphuric acid, soda, bleaching powder and alum. The company was frequently prosecuted for allowing acid fumes to blight the surrounding area. The comprehensive works included furnaces, chambers, towers, a laboratory, an overhead railway and tall chimneys. There were also homes for the foremen on site. The Felling Shore

Next page, clockwise from top left: 1) *Friar's Goose Chemical Works* 2) *The spoil heap of Friar's Goose Chemical Works seen in 1990.* 3) *The chemical works shown on the 1898 Ordnance Survey map.*

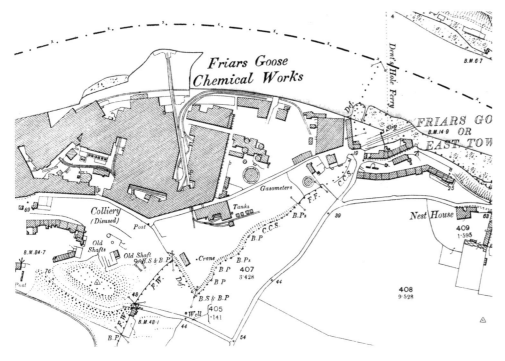

works closed in 1886 with the loss of 1,400 jobs. Today the site is occupied by a modern industrial estate.

In 1822, an alkali works was established by Isaac Cookson at Templetown, Jarrow, largely to supply the glassworks at South Shields. Any surplus alkali was exported. The works closed in 1844 following prosecutions for escaping gas and crop damage. It was soon reopened by a newly formed business, the Jarrow Chemical Company. The works expanded to become the largest chemical factory in the North East and eventually took over the chemical works at Friar's Goose.

The Jarrow Chemical Company had a reputation for being a progressive employer. It financed the building of schools, houses and institutes for workers and their families. The firm introduced half-day working on Saturdays rather than the usual six-day week.

Taken over by the United Alkali Company in 1891, the Jarrow works was immediately closed and demolished to make way for extensions to the Tyne Dock site. Nearby is the Alkali pub building, although no longer used for its original purpose.

Heworth Chemical Works was founded by John Allen and Thomas Coultherd at Heworth Shore in 1828. Eight years later, they took over a collapsed chemical business at the top of nearby Brewery Lane and operated both sites. Allen and Coultherd were the first to import pyrites into the Tyne as a substitute for pure sulphur in the making of sulphuric acid.

The partnership ended in 1847 and John Allen opened a new chemical factory at Wallsend. The Heworth Chemical Works continued to operate until the late 1890s under different owners. The site is today partly covered by an international paint factory.

To the east, at Hebburn, Tennants of Glasgow began producing alkali made from sulphate of soda in 1865. Their Hebburn Alkali Works was just to the west of Hebburn town, near the cross-Tyne ferry to Walker. A 1911 advertisement listed its products as sulphuric acid, hydrochloric acid, hypo, bleaching powder, sodium sulphide, water glass, soda crystals, pearl hardening and satinite. The works declined rapidly after the First World War and today the site is part of Hebburn Riverside Park.

Alan Morgan

Soap

The first important soap factory on Tyneside appears in records from 1790. It stood near the Close Gate in Newcastle, immediately west of the Mayor's residence, the Mansion House and belonged to Doubleday & Easterby. George Doubleday had previously been in partnership with a Mr Fawcett (as soap manufacturers) outside Newcastle's West Gate.

A trade directory of 1827 records Doubleday & Easterby as soap-makers at the Close and as 'Oil of Vitriol' (sulphuric acid) manufacturers at Bill Quay. Around about this time the partners were experimenting with making their own alkali, leading to complaints of unpleasant smells

emanating from the works, affecting people visiting or living in the Mansion House next door.

The Close Gate soap works disappears from trade directories after 1844 and the factory was replaced by the Phoenix Flour Mill in 1855. The site today is covered by modern buildings, including part of the Copthorne Hotel.

Another soap company was founded by Clapham & Forster next to the south east side of the Ouseburn Road Bridge on Byker Bank, Newcastle, in around 1811. In about 1827, Anthony Clapham acquired an additional site at Friar's Goose on the south bank of the Tyne opposite St Peter's. Clapham & Forster disappear from trade directories after 1833. The Ouseburn site later became a pottery, followed by glassworks and other businesses. Today, a timber merchant occupies the location.

One of the most prominent soap works on the Tyne operated in City Road, Newcastle for over 150 years. From a site opposite Gibson Street, the factory reached down towards the river in an area known as the Swirle, named after a burn that issued into the Tyne. It was founded in 1838 by John Greene, who moved his tallow chandler's business here from Gateshead, primarily to meet a huge and growing demand for candles. Thomas Hedley, the son of a Northumbrian sheep farmer and a former junior employee of Greene, was at this stage invited to join the firm as a managing partner. After around twenty years,

Hedley was able to take full control of the soap business and its name changed to Thomas Hedley & Co.

The business prospered, largely due to the lifting of the tax on soap following the cholera outbreak of 1853, and the introduction of palm oil as an alternative to tallow (animal fat) in the manufacturing process. Hedley's company made around fifty types of soap, including pale, brown, cold water, special, mottled and scented. At this stage, most of the output was for the home market. The factory had a fifty-yard frontage on City Road, but by the 1890s it extended significantly to the rear with buildings rising to a maximum of six floors. Hedley was prominent in Newcastle politics – at various times he was Sheriff, Mayor, Alderman and JP. He died in 1890.

Thomas Hedley & Co, City Road, 1890s.

The partnership was replaced by a public limited liability company in 1897. The City Road works launched Fairy Soap in around 1898, the first of several major brands. The Elder Dempster Shipping Company bought a controlling interest in Hedley's in 1900 to guarantee cargoes of African palm oil for their ships. In 1930, Hedley's was acquired by Procter and Gamble, one of America's largest soap manufacturers. In 1990, the company opened a new manufacturing plant in the region at Seaton Delaval where the production of cosmetics and baby-care products continues. Three years later the City Road buildings were demolished to make way for the Sandgate car park and part of the Quayside Highway. The company's offices were subsequently moved from Gosforth to premises at the Cobalt Business Park, North Tyneside.

The term 'soap opera', applied to various long-running TV programmes, owes its origin to Procter & Gamble in America in the 1920s. During this period the company began to advertise its soap products during breaks in the popular radio series *Amos and Andy*. Later, Procter & Gamble sponsored the programme.

There was another soap works on the southern bank of the Tyne at Dunston, Gateshead. This opened in 1909 alongside an earlier flour mill and was owned and operated by the Co-operative Wholesale Society (CWS). The impressive ferro-concrete building was a familiar landmark on the riverside a short distance up river from Dunston Staiths. After the Second World War the soap works became a hide and skin works until the mid-1980s. Today a modern housing estate covers part of the site.

Alan Morgan

Manure

The first Tyneside chemical manure works opened at Blaydon in 1844. In 1877, the firm became the Blaydon Manure and Alkali Co. Ltd., with John Wigham Richardson, the shipbuilder, as chairman. Initially, most of the raw material needed for the business was obtained locally. By the 1870s mineral phosphates from America and Europe began to supplant local material with the possible exception of bones. Sulphuric acid, an essential ingredient of the trade, was largely produced locally but it created environmental problems.

Acid fumes polluted the atmosphere and in 1881 an Act of Parliament was passed to create a team of inspectors to control this contamination. However, the smell from the works and from surrounding trades such as slaughterhouses, bone yards and glue houses was not covered by the 1881 Act.

Local regulations stipulated that no inhabited house should be within two-hundred yards of a manure factory. This rule seems to have been overlooked if the houses were occupied mainly by employees of the manure works. The smell arose from the heaps of fermenting slaughterhouse waste and other offensive materials that were normally left to rot for between five and six months.

Another Newcastle firm involved in this trade was Sampson Langdale of Mushroom Quay, near the glasshouses at St Lawrence. Established in 1849, the firm's site had good wharf and railway facilities and employed at least five-hundred workers during the busy season. The business flourished and declared that 'there is hardly a quarter of the globe into which Langdale's manures and fertilisers have not penetrated'.

Sampson Langdale's remained at Mushroom Quay until it was replaced by the Spillers Flour Mill in 1938, when the works relocated to nearby Bottlehouse Street. The company was absorbed into Fisons Fertiliser Group around 1950 and the business survived until at least 1968. Housing and light industry now cover the former industrial site.

Alan Morgan

Ropes

Tyneside became world renowned for rope-making from the 18th century onwards. Rope 'walks' were a distinctive feature of the early trade. Among the early rope-makers was the Crawhall family, who established their business in 1812 at St Ann's, Newcastle, on the site of a former ropery dating back to at least 1723. The five-acre site was immediately below St Ann's Church on the New Road, later known as City Road.

The three-hundred yard long rope walk, which is marked on James Corbridge's 1723 map, ran along the top of the grassy bank above the North Shore. Before mechanisation, workers walked backwards spinning the hemp and attaching fibres to hooks placed on each of the twenty or so 'hurdles' spaced along the rope walk. At the end of the walk, the workers returned quickly to the start, unhitching the hooks ready to begin walking backwards again. It was a laborious process. Mechanisation of the rope-making process was first successfully accomplished in the 1790s at Sunderland.

Born in Allendale, the son of a lead mining official, Joseph Crawhall was apprenticed as a rope maker to Thomas Smith at the nearby St Peter's shipyard. Crawhall's St Ann's ropery prospered, undertaking work for shipping and colliery companies, and in 1851, the firm was awarded a medal at the Great Exhibition for 'the excellence of their productions'. Crawhall was Mayor of Newcastle in 1849 and as a talented artist he is frequently recorded as 'filling his account books with sketches.'

The works were sold to new owners in 1887 and trade continued to flourish. Orders included work for suspension bridges, overhead railways and cable trams. Exports boomed; one order was for a length of steel wire rope measuring 6,000 yards (three and a half miles) for the Melbourne Cable Tramway Company. In 1912, the business moved to Gateshead where it could expand. A nearby thoroughfare at St Ann's was renamed Crawhall Road.

Another prominent ropery, also founded in the early 1700s, was at St Lawrence, Newcastle, close to St Ann's. Thomas Smith, who was born near Amble in 1757, had been apprenticed here to proprietor, Anthony Pearson. Smith married Pearson's daughter and subsequently inherited the business. Interested in local politics, Smith served twice as Mayor of Newcastle.

In 1810, Thomas Smith, and his two sons, Thomas Jnr. and William, also began a shipbuilding business at St Peter's, taking over the former shipyard of William Rowe, while continuing to operate their ropery at nearby St Lawrence. Ropes for deep-sea dredging were a speciality. The firm fitted out the ship *Discovery* used by Captain Scott on his first visit to the Antarctic and in the 1920s it supplied the wire ropes used in the erection of the Sydney Harbour Bridge. The business became a founder member of British Ropes in 1924.

The site is part of today's modern developments around St Peter's Basin which include street names such as The Ropery, Rowe's Mews and Bottlehouse Street.

In 1789, retired sea captain William Chapman established a ropery at Willington Quay on the banks of Willington Gut, a tributary of the Tyne. Following Chapman's death in 1793, his sons, William (later to be better known as a canal and harbour engineer) and Edward, carried on the business. In 1797, they patented a machine that could make rope of any length without a splice.

Chapman's Willington Quay ropery became well known, especially for producing long hemp ropes for inclined waggonways such as those used to transport coal. Many of their ropes were used by the Navy, including Nelson's fleet at the Battle of Trafalgar in 1805. Young George Stephenson, who lived nearby for a while, operated the ropery engine when its attendant fell sick.

Robert Hood Haggie took over the lease of Chapman's Ropery in 1843, having left his own family's ropery at the South Shore, Gateshead following a family dispute. Robert and his family eventually moved into Low Willington Villa, near the former Chapman works, which in later years served as the works canteen.

Haggie's Willington Quay Ropery was devastated by fire in 1873, but most of the works were rebuilt and modernised in preparation for the increased production of binder twine. Haggie's 'Robin Hood' and 'Rob Roy' brands of twine were sold world-wide as reaping machines became popular with farmers. The business specialised in fibre ropes until 1885 and then switched to steel wire ones, which were in great demand from shipping and mining companies. Haggie's products were used in the diamond mines of South Africa. British Ropes, of Doncaster, took over Haggie's business in 1959 and today the Bridon Group continues to manufacture a wide range of high tensile wire products at the Willington Quay site.

The earliest evidence of rope-making on the South Shore at Gateshead dates to 1782 when there are references to 'Harvey's raff yard, east end of rope walk' and 'Edward Softley, publican, Rope-makers, South Shore'. In 1795, there is also a reference to the 'Gateshead Ropery, Stoddart & Co., Saltmeadows'.

Some time before 1811, David Haggie, father of Robert Hood Haggie, was taken into partnership by Anthony Hood, owner of another ropery, on the South Shore for the business to become known as Hood & Haggie Rope Makers. Later, David Haggie and Peter Hood, brother of Anthony, became brothers in law.

By 1819, David Haggie was in partnership with James Pollard of Newcastle, making ropes on the South Shore in a business known as Pollard, Haggie and Co. During the early 1830s, the firm's name changed to David Haggie & Son. The son taken into partnership was Robert Hood Haggie. Products of the South Shore works were sold to mining, shipping and railway companies. In the early 1840s the business made a 'monster line' for an inclined plane on the Liverpool to Manchester Railway, which was three miles long and weighed thirteen imperial tons.

Following the retirement of David Haggie in 1842, two of his youngest sons, Peter and David Junior, joined their elder brother Robert as partners in the business which prompted Robert to resign and take over Chapman's Ropery at Willington Quay. Peter became manager of the South Shore works at the age of twenty-two, while his elder brother, David, focused on local politics and became Mayor of Gateshead in 1853. David was very much involved in dealing with the after-effects of the Great Fire of Gateshead the following year, including the transformation of part of the ropery buildings into a temporary refuge for the homeless.

At Haggie's South Shore Ropery in the 1840s men and boys started work at 5am (6.30am in winter), and the ten-hour day included fifteen minutes for breakfast with thirty minutes for dinner. Most work was in the open air. Candles or artificial light were not allowed; boys earned 3s. to 4s. 6d. per week and bound apprentices 5s. to 7s. per week.

In 1924, Haggie Brothers became a founder member of British Ropes. The works closed in 1962, today there are no buildings on the site of the former ropery, between The Sage Gateshead and the Baltic Centre for Contemporary Art.

Two roperies were formed at Low Teams, Gateshead in around 1840. The first was set up shortly before 1840 by John Dixon, the son of a local coal owner (who was also one of the best known of the early railway engineers under

George Stephenson) and John Corbitt, who belonged to a family of Gateshead ropemakers. The Dixon & Corbitt works on the east side of the Team (a tributary of the Tyne), introduced the earliest machinery in the district to produce manila hemp ropes from finely spun yarns, suitable for yachts, the Royal Navy and merchant ships. At least four-hundred workers were employed, and in 1877 Dixon, also a prominent civil engineer and contractor, devised the air-tight steel cylinder and made the hefty wire cables used to float and tow Cleopatra's Needle from Egypt to London.

The second ropery was founded by Robert Stirling Newall from Dundee, the son of a textile manufacturer, who arrived on Tyneside aged twenty-nine. He patented his invention of untwisted wire rope in 1840 and set up business with two partners on the west bank of the River Team, opposite the Dixon & Corbitt works. Newall's moved into the new manufacturing field of submarine cables, where copper telegraph cables, insulated with gutta-percha were encased in wire rope to protect them as they lay on the sea bed. The fibre cores for Newall's wire ropes were supplied by Dixon & Corbitt.

In 1887, both of the Team's rope works amalgamated, and then around 1900 the Newall rope works moved to Liverpool following quarrels between the respective families and a slump in manufacturing. The remaining business was finally absorbed into Britsh Ropes in 1926 and then transferred to the Hood Haggie site at Willington Quay, twenty years later. Both sites at Low Teams have been partially replaced by light industry with the remainder of the area awaiting redevelopment.

Alan Morgan

In 1843, Robert Hood Haggie acquired and developed this site near Willington Quay, close to the railway viaduct of 1839. At this time, only natural fibre ropes were manufactured; however, as the mining industry in the North East of England flourished, the demand for longer lasting, stronger ropes increased. In 1885, wire ropes began to be produced at Willington Quay.

Pottery

Although Tyneside potteries had access to cheap coal and brown clay the region lacked the quality clays found elsewhere in England. These finer clays, plus other materials such as flint, usually arrived on Tyneside (at little cost to the manufacturer) as ballast in the holds of sailing colliers returning for more coal. Following the demise of these vessels raw materials were then imported by more modern transport which incurred a greater charge.

During the period of nearly 250 years that the pottery industry flourished on Tyneside, at least one-hundred different firms had been involved in the trade. The first recorded pottery in the area was situated at Pandon Dean (now covered by Manors Metro Station) where in around 1730 John Warburton from Staffordshire set up a business to manufacture brown-ware. About ten years later at a subsequent pottery at Gateshead, Warburton was the first in the district to produce white-wares largely as a result of an earlier discovery that by adding powdered flint to the clay mix a satisfactory whiteness could be achieved as well as a more robust product.

By 1827, there were around twenty potteries on Tyneside several of which were in the Ouseburn valley. Traditional working methods continued well into the 1800s often due to workers fear of redundancy if machinery was adopted. The first known machine was introduced in 1833 for roller-printing but within another forty years or so machines were widespread. Most Tyneside pottery was produced for the middle to lower end of the market and rarely equalled the quality of pottery manufactured in Staffordshire, Worcester or London. By the mid-19th century there were fewer but larger and more efficient potteries, one of which was run by the Maling family at Ouseburn.

The Maling family had escaped religious persecution in France during the 16th century to settle as merchants in East Yorkshire before moving to Sunderland to set up as potters in 1762. The business was then transferred to Tyneside where a pottery opened at Ouseburn Bridge in 1815. In 1859, and with the help of a generous dowry, the recently married Christopher Thompson Maling masterminded the construction of a state of the art replacement pottery on a nearby two acre site that became over fifty times more productive than at Ouseburn Bridge. This new pottery in Ford Street was named the Ford Pottery after the maiden name of his wife Mary Ford. At least ninety percent of the output were earthenware jam and preserve pots for the wholesale commercial market that included Keiller's of Dundee, the well-known makers of jams and marmalade.

In 1879 Malings opened a second purpose built pottery to cope with a surge in demand for products on a fourteen acre site less than a mile away that required the huge investment of around £100,000. At around twelve times more productive than the earlier Ford A pottery, this new Ford B factory was thought to have been the largest pottery on one site in the UK and probably in the world at that time. Self-sufficient, except for some raw material, it was also ideally situated alongside a railway and close to a riverside quay. Manufacturing processes were dovetailed

Top: *The Ford B Pottery was completed in 1879, the buildings covered an area of six and half acres.*
Bottom: *Female workers at Malings, 1930s.*

for greater efficiency and in addition, social facilities existed by way of a school for the children of employees, a chapel, a soup kitchen and allotments.

For several decades thereafter both potteries prospered and at their peak employed over one-thousand workers. However, trading conditions deteriorated after World War One and Ford A was forced to close in 1927 followed by Ford B in 1963. A scrap metal business now occupies the site of the Ford A pottery and small independent firms operate in most of the remaining buildings once occupied by Ford B.

Apart from Maling's two factories the only other Tyneside pottery to survive World War One was the firm of Adamsez Ltd that began as Adams & Co in 1880 near Scotswood Bridge. They specialised in sanitary ware using fireclay from a local clay pit. Fireclay was usually found beneath coal seams and originated as soil in which prehistoric forests grew and later compacted by pressure and heat. Diversification occurred in 1904 into garden ornaments, cemetery memorials and smaller household items until the business closed in 1972. A small industrial estate with Adamsez incorporated into its title now covers the site.

Other than some remaining parts of former potteries at Walker Road (Ford B) and Stepney Bank (John Wood and Co) there are no other visible reminders of this once important pottery industry except for street names. Pottery Lane continues near the Metro Radio Arena and at St Anthony's there is Pottery Bank. Some examples of local pottery can be seen at nearby museums and art galleries.

Alan Morgan

Paper

Paper is a matted or felted sheet, usually made of cellulose fibres suspended in water and then formed on a wire screen. Paper making, whereby disintegrated rags were felted to produce paper, was first practised in China in about AD 105, but it would seem that it was not until the 14th century that this method came to be used in parts of Europe. The invention of the printing press in about 1450 greatly increased the demand for paper, and this may have been the catalyst for the earliest known British paper mill – John Tate's 1495 'Sele Mill' at Stevenage. Tate employed what was by then a well-developed continental system of paper making, using water powered stamps (hammers) for the initial maceration of the rags to produce a pulp. This was the third industrial use for the water wheel, after corn milling and the fulling of wool, but it remained the only part of the paper-making process to be mechanised until the early 1800s, when paper was first made by machine. Thus, all paper made before the end of the 18th century, was hand-made in vat mills, so called because the pulp was transferred to a vat – a circular cross-section wooden tub in which the sheets of paper were made by hand using a 'mould' of fine wire 'cloth' fixed in a stiff wooden frame.

In around 1798, the French engineer Nicholas-Louis Robert constructed the first paper-making machine, with a moving screen belt, and a few years later the brothers Henry and Sealy Fourdrinier, both British paper-makers, improved Robert's device, and paper machines were thereafter known as 'Fourdriniers'. The early machines were only four to five feet wide, producing papers of that width, but by the 1830s, a Scotswood-on-Tyne paper mill had two machines of ninety-four inches wide, and by the 1860s, machines of more than a hundred inches wide were becoming common.

Although almost all steps in papermaking had now become mechanised, the basic process remained essentially unchanged. First, the macerated raw material fibres were wetted to produce the paper pulp, or stock. The pulp was then filtered on a woven screen to form a sheet of fibre which was pressed and compacted to squeeze out most of the water. The remaining water was removed by evaporation, and the dry sheet was further compressed and, depending upon the intended use, coated or impregnated with other substances. The best quality white papers, for writing and printing, were made from linens and cotton. The poorer quality brown and blue papers, for wrapping and packaging, were made from poorer rags, rope, canvas, netting, etc. It seems at least possible that the emergence of the once familiar Rag and Bone men, was a response to the paper industry's need for rags for making paper, and bones for making glue size for sizing it.

Reliable water supplies were needed for water-powered mills, but clean water was also needed for pulping and washing. Consequently, paper milling became an essentially rural industry before the advent of steam power, although one preferably located near important markets such as towns or universities, or near established ports with easy access to such markets.

It may be thought relevant that the first ever provincial newspaper was produced in a shop on the old Tyne Bridge in 1639, by the 'King's Travelling Printer', but this pre-dates any known north-eastern paper mill. However, the North East was quite well suited to a paper making industry. It had a reasonable local market, the import of raw materials was fairly straightforward, while exporting was just as easy, there were sufficient rivers suitable for water power, and later it was an ideal area for the application of steam power. It also had related industries in ropemaking, providing a useful raw material, and in the chemical industry for bleaches. In fact, North East England became famous for its 'Newcastle Browns', (also known as 'Rope Browns' or 'Tyne Casings') long before the beer of that name was produced, and the coarser, tougher papers became a north-east speciality.

The earliest known, paper mills in the North East were at Croxdale (1678), Chopwell (1697), and Lintz (c.1703), all in County Durham, but 18th century expansion was relatively slow – Gibside (1728-80), Hawks at Felling Shore (c.1750s), Fourstones (1762/3), Haughton (1788), and Relly (by 1798). However, the introduction of steam-powered paper-making machines saw a considerable expansion in north-east paper-making in the 19th century, at Shotley Bridge, Scotswood, Deptford in Sunderland, South Hylton and Jarrow for example, all before 1840. The creation of these mills demonstrates the new importance of steam power, sea transport, effluent disposal, and port-based locations.

As competition between the old hand-made and new machine-made paper makers became intense, many hand makers could only survive financially by neglecting to pay the duties levied on the manufacture of paper. This was a potentially imprisonable offence, and it has been alleged that in around 1825-26, only two of the twelve or so paper makers in the North East were at liberty.

The excise on paper was reformed in 1839, but not abolished, and a duty of 1½d per pound was placed on all paper, irrespective of its quality, or of the raw materials used in the making of brown paper. The duties were not entirely repealed until 1860. Now much jute waste, from sugar and cotton baggings, began to be used locally. This enabled the North East's brown paper makers, in particular, to expand, and to use, as raw materials, old railway waggon covers, straw, tarpaulins, old door mats, etc. – anything made of fibre that was cheap and could be readily reduced to a pulp.

The first patent for using Esparto grass in paper making was taken out in 1839, but its first commercially successful use in paper manufacture was by Thomas Routledge, who took out three relevant patents in around 1855. In around 1862, Routledge took over Ford (Hylton) Paper Mill on the south bank of the Wear near Sunderland, and here he introduced his Esparto grass method for the manufacture of printing papers, the first time it had been used on a large scale, Hylton Mill thus became the first fully developed plant for the conversion of Esparto grass into white paper. By 1864, nearly all news-print paper, including that of *The Times*, incorporated Esparto grass.

The North East was ideally placed to import Esparto grass. Ships from the North East took coal and coke to Spain, mainly for lead ore smelters, and often brought back heavier mineral ores, for example manganese, pyrites, galena, copper etc. as ballast, together with a near-full cargo of the very light Esparto grass freighted on top of the minerals, virtually free of transport charges. As the rivers Tyne and Wear became leading importers and re-exporters of Esparto grass, paper makers in Edinburgh and Lancashire obtained their Esparto grass from the North East by rail. Another result of this trade was a growing concentration of paper mills at ports, or at locations with good rail links to ports. The introduction of Esparto grass was all the more welcome, for it coincided with a cotton famine and a resultant scarcity of wastes from the cotton mills. It also tied in with other basic north-eastern industries for the grass was treated with soda ash and considerable amounts of bleaching powder, both of which were readily available from the North East's alkali works. New north-eastern paper mills were established for Esparto grass paper, and although some, such as those at Morpeth and Bedlington, had short lives, others lasted well into the 20th century – Team Valley (1868-1965), Hendon (1872c.-2005), Hartlepool (1891c.-1960s).

The first commercial plant for wood-pulp paper had opened in Germany in 1846, and the first United Kingdom wood-pulp paper mill was established in Kent in 1886. By the 1890s, the trade in Esparto and rags had been outstripped by imports of wood-pulp. Esparto's reign was threatened, but it was not until the early 1970s that it was well and truly over.

Only a few new works were established in the North East in the twentieth century, for example the small works of Pembertons in Gateshead, established in 1922 in a former tannery building to utilise waste paper. More significantly, Kimberly Clark commenced at Prudhoe in 1971, producing crepe tissue from North American and Scandinavian wood pulp, and the works continues in production. But overall, the pattern through the 20th century was mainly one of closures.

As might be expected, water-powered paper mills could suffer from the extremes of the elements, and many were damaged in that way, by wind and water, but fire was the greatest threat, whether the mill was powered by water or steam, for they always contained an abundance of combustible materials – rags, tarred rope, paper, dry grass, etc. Thus, on 14 August 1826, a newly erected paper mill at Scotswood was on fire, and soon, because of the nature of the materials, the premises were a heap of ruins. Nearby hedges, a coal staith, cottages and a coal tar manufactory were ignited as burning sheets of paper flew around. Similarly, on 6 February 1846, Hutton Fletcher & Co's extensive Ayres Quay (Sunderland) Paper Mill was completely burnt down, its workmen had been on strike for three weeks and arson was suspected. On 9 August in the following year, Nathaniel Grace's Scotswood Paper Mill was entirely destroyed by fire; the fire was said to have blazed with great fury, and attracted spectators for miles around.

There are, of course, interesting stories behind many of the North East's paper mills, but space does not allow an examination of them all. Consequently only a few will be discussed below.

Fourstones Paper Mill was founded in 1762/3, as a water-powered vat mill, it was the first paper mill in Northumberland. After some troubled decades the mill was sold to Alexander Adam in 1865, and he introduced the use of Esparto grass. After a several more changes in ownership the mill was taken over in 1962 by a Czech entrepreneur, Mr George T Mandl, who had fled the communists in his homeland in 1949, arriving in London with the proverbial £2 10s in his pocket. But with a family background in the paper industry, he soon took a position with the Buckingham Paper & Box Co in West Drayton, before establishing his own 'London Boxboard Co', a one-man agency business which he built up into an international concern. This led him to acquire a majority interest in the Fourstones Mill in 1962, and he later acquired other mills in Britain and Europe. Fourstones Paper Mill is still in business (2015) on possibly the longest surviving paper mill site in the United Kingdom.

Haughton Castle Paper Mill, on the North Tyne, was established by Captain William Smith of Haughton Castle in 1788, as a water-powered vat mill. Smith was to become known as 'Buccaneer Smith' after he offered to store arms, with which volunteers could defend the country against Napoleon, at the castle. But his actual involvement with Napoleon was of quite a different order. In around 1793, with France under its Revolutionary Government, Prime Minister Pitt ordered an immense number of French Assignats (the French Revolutionary Government's paper money) to be made in England, and distributed throughout France in an attempt to devalue the Government's currency. Three English paper mills were chosen to make the paper, one of these being that at Haughton. Examples of French watermarks were given to the three mills, as well as examples of the paper money, and by the Autumn of 1793, Haughton had been making nothing but these Assignats 'for months', sending up to ninety reams of paper to London per week by mail coach. In 1795, manufacture of Assignat Paper was quietly dropped at Haughton.

Four years later Haughton Paper Mill was taken over by Alexander and John Annandale, members of a Scottish paper-making family. The Annandales held Haughton Mill for twenty-one years, but they then wished to fry bigger fish, having bought the Shotley Grove estate in County Durham in 1812 where they established a very large new paper mill. Although their first mill at Shotley Bridge was clearly a vat mill, the Annandales acquired three paper machines between 1829 and 1835 from a seemingly unlikely supplier – Robert Stephenson & Co. of Newcastle – as well as hydraulic presses from the same company. By 1895, Annandale was one of the largest paper manufacturers in the Kingdom, and four years later the

works was employing some three hundred people, half of whom were girls and young women, sorting rags, picking Esparto, etc. But the entire works was offered for sale in 1903, at a time when it only had three machines at work. Whether it was bought is not known, but the works closed down in around 1910, presumably because of its isolation from the ports, and the fact that while the Derwent Valley Railway had been important to it, the works were over a mile from the line.

There were two paper mills at Scotswood-on-Tyne, one owned by William Grace & Co. which was steam-powered by 1825, the other, originally powered by the Denton Burn before becoming steam-powered in 1812, was in the ownership of Thomas Ramsay by 1825. This mill is of particular interest because it was visited by Commissioner Leifchild for the 1842 enquiry into the *Employment and Condition of Children in Mines and Manufactories*. By then, the proprietor was named as Mr Ramsay, aged twenty-eight, who had lived there for twenty years. The paper mill, with two paper machines, was employing fourteen young men, twenty-one 'female young persons', six male children, two female children, and an unspecified number of adults. Ramsay also noted that twelve to fourteen workers at the mill had some of their children working there.

Leifchild's interviews with some of the girls working at the mill provide information that is very difficult, if not impossible, to obtain elsewhere. Elizabeth Jobling, aged sixteen had worked there for two years. In her first year she had worked on 'Long Elephant' paper. She cut sheets of paper twelve yards long; this paper was produced by machine, then wound off a drum by the girls, laid on a table twelve yards long, and then cut into twelve yard pieces by a knife. When Elizabeth was working at this job, her shifts varied between five and eight hours on six days a week, and she was paid 9d. for every ten hours worked. In her second year she was put on rag cutting and was presently cutting old bagging and sacking for 10d. per hundredweight. Sometimes she did night work, for example scraping old rope to get the tar out after it had been boiled. She had spent only three or four months at a school, could only read her letters, and could not write at all.

Isabella Henderson, aged nearly nine years, took the 'sheets out of the glazing boards'. She usually commenced work at 5am and always finished at 8pm. Breakfast was brought to the mill by her brother at 8am, and she had thirty minutes to eat it, likewise dinner at 12 noon, and bread, butter and tea at 5.30pm Except for these breaks she had to stand all day, and she 'felt very sleepy at night'. She earned 3s. per week, for a six-day week. Like Elizabeth Jobling, she could only read her letters, and could not write at all, but she attended Bell's Close Methodist Chapel every Sunday, both at Sunday school and in the evening.

Some young girls regularly mixed day shifts with night shifts, the night shift being 6pm to 6am. At busy times, many girls worked from 8am until 2am on the following day. One boy of about nineteen years regularly stoked boilers for eighty-six hours per week for 15s. 8d. per week, and once worked twenty-nine hours non-stop. Ramsay argued that these long hours were a result of the children expecting to earn a certain amount in a day, and given the accepted hourly rates of pay, this made long hours inevitable.

The Commission reports make us appreciate the significant contribution made by children to the progress of the Industrial Revolution in the North East and elsewhere, but they also give us reason to reflect on similar dependencies in today's 'emerging' countries like India and Bangladesh.

Stafford M. Linsley

Next page clockwise from top left: 1) *The former drying loft at Haughton Paper Mill, photographed in 1973.*
2) *An illustration of the Shotley Grove paper mills from* The History and Biography of West Durham *(Consett, 1881 or 1883).*
3) *The former Barrasford Paper Mill.*

Agriculture

The first half of the 18th century in England witnessed a growth in the movement of outside capital into agriculture. It also saw some improvements in transport, navigations and turnpikes – and a consequent growth in inter-regional trade, as well as net exports of grain. But England was not yet a land of advanced agriculture and transport systems.

Some of the best corn lands were still unenclosed, and in such cases medieval, if not Anglo-Saxon methods of farming still held sway on vast, hedge-less open fields. In parts of North East England much land was vastly under-utilised, while many cattle were still being slaughtered and salted, as there was insufficient hay to keep them through the winter. But better farming methods were known, and by the middle of the century, with a 'Spirit of Improvement' very much in the air, better agricultural practices were being instituted. This was manifested in extensive enclosures, (often of former commons and wastes, transforming formerly barren, almost wilderness areas into profitable arable and pastoral lands), and in improved farming methods and implements.

The causes, nature and overall impact of this Age of (Agricultural) Improvement, circa 1750-1815, are not entirely clear, and in that respect it is rather like the Industrial Revolution, a process rather than an event. Thus the agricultural history of Northumberland in this period, is unlikely to be the same as Norfolk's; indeed it is unlike that of Durham and Cleveland. Part of the reason for such differences is explained by the landowning pattern in Northumberland – a very important factor in its agricultural development.

The pattern of land ownership, and farm size, is a unique feature of Northumberland, as statistics from 1833 demonstrate. These figures gave the proportion of land, excluding 'wastes', in each English county that was owned by landowners who held, individually, more than 10,000 acres. Ignoring the aberrant figures for the small county of Rutland, some fifty per cent of Northumberland was so owned, easily the highest percentage in the country. In addition, Northumberland had fifty-two per cent of its holdings at over five-hundred acres (against a national average of some twenty-four per cent) and twenty-four per cent over 1,000 acres, again both easily the highest figures for any English county. These figures demonstrate the dominance of large landowners in Northumberland, and indicate how they could, if they so wished, change the face of the county's agriculture. In County Durham, by contrast, only twenty-eight per cent of its holdings exceeded 10,000 acres. Most farms in County Durham, historically, were between fifty and one-hundred and fifty acres, and a great many were less than fifty acres, many of its farm buildings being a hotch-potch, often crudely put together with minimal capital expenditure. Such farms can only be unfavourably compared with the splendid planned farmsteads of Northumberland, but there are long-understood reasons for this situation. John Bailey in 1810, attributed the poor quality of Durham farmsteads to two basic factors. Firstly Durham's farms were generally small in acreage, but secondly and more importantly, potential tenants were only offered short leases, a clear deterrent to any ambitious farmer.

The great estates of north eastern landowners were units of political and economic power, but politics aside, the most obvious avenue for a landlord's influence was in agriculture. Some chose to exercise this power, others did not – the Dukes of Northumberland, for example, before 1847, were probably the least enterprising landlords in the

Rural life in Teesdale.

north, although their performance improved under the fourth Duke. However, in general, agricultural improvement became something of a craze during the second half of the 18th century, but one that could yield considerable profits, for improved farming meant business-like farming, a reasonably profitable economic proposition. Nationally, however, agricultural improvement had also become a necessity, for a rising population was increasing the demand for meat and wheat as a result of the growth of towns, factories and the non-agricultural population. Moreover, England ceased to be a net corn-exporting country from about 1780, and therefore, if the non-agricultural population was to be fed without recourse to imports, agriculture needed to be considerably reformed.

Traditionally, in explaining the agrarian transformation of the 18th century, the accent has been on certain landlords and others who introduced 'new' agricultural methods – people like Coke of Norfolk, 'Turnip' Townshend, Jethro Tull, etc. – a 'heroic' interpretation of the transformation. But such accounts have been much revised in recent decades, it being noted, for example, that Coke's much vaunted Norfolk four-course rotation was never popular, and indeed had been abandoned in Norfolk by the mid-19th century. As in so many other areas of economic life, the best practitioners were pragmatic, and the best farmers developed their crop rotations to suit their soils and climate. So, while there was an agrarian transformation, it was wrought by 'practical farmers', a term used at the time by those who had little inclination to listen to 'gentleman farmers'. The 'Age of Improvement' was primarily concerned with more productive farming and concomitant higher farm incomes and rents, and it brought unprecedented prosperity to some farming communities.

A key region in the developments of this period was north Northumberland, where the much-admired 'Northumberland System of Husbandry', based on the careful cultivation and use of turnips (instead of bare fallows) and of 'artificial grasses', was brought to a high art, a centre of excellence – 'a complete revolution in the management and value of land' according to John Grey of Dilston, Receiver for the Greenwich Hospital Estates in the north (1841). And as T. L. Colbeck was to write (1847):

With little fear of contradiction ... no portion of England has made such rapid improvement within the last forty years as Northumberland ... We have no hesitation in attributing this improvement mainly to the improved turnip husbandry, as the increase in cattle is in the face of many thousand acres of grassland having been brought under the plough; thus proving the striking fact, that we now can, with much less grassland than formerly, actually feed more cattle, as well as grow more corn.

Particularly influential in those parts of Northumberland that had achieved that elevated status, and not all of them had done so, were the most celebrated 'practical farmers' in North East England – the Culley brothers. George (1735 -1813) and Matthew Culley (1731-1804), were born at Denton, near Darlington, to a small landed family. They were related to the Colling family, and Matthew was to marry into the Bates family; both of these families were renowned for their efforts to improve shorthorn cattle. It was Charles Colling of Brafferton, near Darlington, who bred the famous Durham Ox, sold in 1801 to a Lincolnshire farmer for £250, and subsequently toured around the country on exhibition.

In 1762, while still quite young men, George and Matthew had been sent to study under Robert Bakewell at Dishley, Leicestershire, and George in particular became convinced of the merits of the selective cross-breeding of sheep. He went on to produce what became known as the 'Culley' breed, and eventually as the 'Border Leicester'. The Culley brothers moved to Fenton in Glendale, Northumberland, in 1767, as tenant farmers, and introduced the breed to Northumberland to stand beside and compete with breeds such as the 'Cheviot' breed of the hills, and the 'Blackface' breed on the higher lands of the South. The Culley breed gave a mutton which seemingly was not palatable to genteel tastes, but it was a cheap mutton, ideal for the growing industrial populations of Tyneside, where the collier ships in particular were victualled with 'Coal Heavers Mutton'.

The brothers had travelled a lot in their early days, but soon 'From every county of the Kingdom, and from every civilised part of Europe and the New World, pupils and strangers crowded to see the scenes of their active and successful labours'. Their sheep-and-turnip system of husbandry had made both the Glendale area and the Culleys themselves famous. By 1801, the Culleys were making annual profits of £9000 from eight farms with a total rental of £5000.

Although there were several improvements to farm implements in the second half of the 18th century, probably the most important of these for North East England, was the fixed barn-threshing machine. Before 1780, all threshing was done by hand, mainly by flail, drudgery of epic proportions for thousands of farm labourers throughout the nation. But an effective threshing machine was developed by Andrew Meikle in the East Lothians in 1786, and some agricultural areas quickly adopted it, while others did not. Its primary advantage was that while one corn stack threshed by flail occupied one man for two weeks, two men with a threshing machine could do it in one day. Even so, while there is widespread evidence for its rapid adoption in the north east of England, there is extremely little evidence for its use in the south of Yorkshire, even though grain production generally increased across the country after 1750, presumably straining available manual sources for threshing in many areas.

Although the threshing machine was not invented in Northumberland, most of the early near-successful experiments were carried out in that county, and it seems possible that these trials ultimately led to the successful machine. As usual, the precise steps towards its development are unclear, and there was much contemporary argument regarding priority of claim to its invention, but it is probably fairly credited to Meikle, no doubt building upon earlier attempts by himself and others.

Uniform rotary motion was important for the threshing machine's efficient operation, hence the prime mover for the machine had itself to be able to maintain a uniform rotary motion. At the time of Meikles's invention, three prime movers were available – the waterwheel, the windmill and the horsewheel, and soon after there was a fourth – the stationary steam engine. The waterwheel came to be quite widely used in north Northumberland and along the Tyne valley, the windmill was only rarely used, steam engines were used in some of the region's coal mining districts, but the horsewheel, more commonly referred to as a Gin-Gan, became the most widely used prime mover for threshing machines in North East England. The spread of the threshing machine in the North East was quite remarkable. In 1794 it was said that they had 'become general in the Northern parts of Northumberland', and in 1799, that they had 'spread over all the corn counties of Scotland and have lately been successfully introduced into the Northern Counties of England, though strange to tell, they are scarcely known in the southern and best cultivated parts.'

There would appear to be one primary reason for this asymmetry, usefully summed up by John Wilkie of Hetton, County Durham, in 1791: 'In this country [area] where hands are scarce [the threshing machine] is particularly useful, there being full employment in the fields for those who used to thresh'. Similarly, Stephen Watson of Cleadon, giving his reasons for installing a threshing machine, noted in 1791:

I am situated in the centre, betwixt two navigable rivers and it is with great difficulty I can get a man to turn his hand to husbandry, as they can make so much greater wages, in a few hours, at either of the ports, by casting of coal into ships and ballast out.

So the threshing machine was welcomed with open arms where labour, mainly male, was scarce, and therefore costly. In the north, there was competition for labour as industrial demands were increasing, hence the rapid adoption of the threshing machine. In much of the south of the country, where employment outside of agriculture was frequently scarce, unskilled labour remained cheap, and consequently the use of the threshing machine would only have been of marginal value. The South therefore continued, happily or unhappily, with the flail, for fifty years after it had largely been abandoned in the North. In 1842, John Grey noted this asymmetry in the national take-up of the threshing machine but attributed it to a lack of native intelligence on the part of southerners:

I know nothing better calculated to preserve the vacant mind in a state of stationary vacuity than the sober sameness of the flail's evolution from morn to night and from week to week ... the man who wields the flail by mere animal strength must undergo much cultivation, and be greatly elevated in mind and acquirements, ere he can become the machine maker.

The other obvious impact of the use of the fixed barn-threshing machine was in farmstead design, and during the second half of the 18th century and the first half of the 19th century, many completely new farmsteads were built throughout the North East region, but particularly in Northumberland. These new steadings were often very carefully planned to incorporate the latest ideas in improved agricultural practice and, after about 1790, their layouts usually hinged on the incorporation of the fixed barn thresher – the focal point of farmstead design.

But the opportunities for better paid non-farm work for males in the North East England also led to higher farm-worker wages. J. Caird, in his 1851 survey of English agriculture, clearly attributed the high wages of male farmworkers in the North of England to labour shortages due to the attraction of the mining industries for many such potential workers. Moreover, as the 'new' farming of the second half of the 18th century needed quite large labour forces, competition for labour between agriculture and other industries meant that in Northumberland, to a greater extent than anywhere else in the kingdom, the shortfall in male agricultural workers was made up by the employment of large numbers of women, including 'bondagers'.

The bondager system, by which farm hinds were normally required under their annual contracts, to provide one or more women workers, often a wife, daughter or sister, but sometimes an 'unattached' female, was certainly common in Northumberland from the second half of the 18th century. The bondager would live with the hind and his family while she worked for a day wage (commonly 1s. per day at harvest and 8d. otherwise by the early nineteenth century). The bondager's money payments were, however, paid to the hind, who in any case provided the bondager's keep, for the bondager was 'bound' to the hind rather than the employing farmer. Bondagers became crucially important to Northumberland agriculture as more and more men left the land to work in coal mines, where few, if any, women had been employed underground after the middle of the 18th century. As Tessa Gray maintained (1984):

Whether Northumberland women enjoyed farm work or not, they had little opportunity for alternative employment. During the eighteenth and nineteenth centuries Newcastle was the only nearby town capable of offering significant opportunities in domestic service. There was no large, local textile industry and none of the out-work industries such as button making, straw plaiting and lace making which gave employment to women in other agricultural districts. Not only did farmers have to employ women, but most women in rural Northumberland had to do farm work if they were to work at all. Northumberland farmers were not alone in seeing the advantages of a cheap, adaptable work force, available when needed but making few demands when unemployed.

Large numbers of women day-workers were also often involved in local agriculture. A list of casual workers at Flodden on the Ford estate in 1766, includes fourteen men and fifteen women, while at Lookout Farm, Hartley, thirty-one women were paid for raking in 1758, and twenty-nine women and one man were paid for shearing corn at 4d. per day in 1759. Women on these farms were also paid for stoning, weeding, binding corn, winnowing, spreading manure, hoeing turnips, and dressing corn, but no indication has yet been found to suggest that women performed the tasks of hedge setting or ploughing. In no other part of the country were so many women employed in agriculture in the 18th and 19th centuries. By the 1890s, the Northumberland women field workers accounted for one-eighth of the national total of women farm workers. So, for Northumberland at least, we cannot in truth describe its farming areas as 'man-made landscapes'.

Stafford M. Linsley

This glass slide shows a picturesque country landscape. Taken in 1928 by South Shields Photographic Society's photographer Harrison Burgess. (TWAM)

Case study: Lowick, North Northumberland

In the 1970s, explorative drilling revealed the existence of sufficient quantities of coal near the village of Lowick to make open-cast mining feasible. The excavation operation went ahead, massive bulldozers and heavy wagons digging out the site, near to the Devil's Causeway (the former Roman road), north of the village. This was just a field away from where two shafts for the Lickar Lea Colliery had been sunk in the early 19th century.

The coal extraction proceeded, using heavy machinery unimaginable to earlier miners, when one of the bulldozers struck something. Most drivers would probably have ignored the obstruction. In this case, however, the bulldozer was stopped and the driver climbed down from his cab to examine what was on the ground.

What he discovered was a miner's shovel lying in the remains of a low tunnel with a pile of gorse beside it. The evidence suggesting the miner was lying on his back to excavate a low seam of coal, probably using a pick and shovel to do so and the gorse, (not the most comfortable back rest) serving as support as he worked.

What you notice first on the photograph is the broad metal section with the rim nearest to the shaft turned upwards to ensure that the coal will remain on the shovel, as the miner makes the sweeping motion necessary to transfer the load into a container, probably some kind of wagon beside him. (The damage on the nearside of the shovel shows the impact of the bulldozer).

The shovel has a rather makeshift appearance, suggesting the miner has gone to the village blacksmith to have the metal beaten into a shape to correspond to his specific requirements. The miner is likely to have fashioned the piece of wood himself, perhaps selecting a suitable branch from an ash tree in one of the nearby woods. The cross-handle section at the end of the shaft, forming the hand-hold, is attached with a simple wooden peg. The shaft is bent out of shape, through the exertions of the miner,

and there is some discolouring at the edge of the shaft from the long period the shovel spent lying buried underground.

What happened to make this unknown miner abandon his shovel – a valuable piece of equipment – we can never know, perhaps a rock fall or some unexpected event leading him to leave suddenly, getting away from the narrow, confining space

The shovel had lain undisturbed underground for more than a hundred years before the miner's world was unexpectedly revealed through modern open-cast mining operations. In itself, a miner's shovel may appear unimportant, one of several surviving from this period. It begins to have significance because of where it was found, the particular context and narrative it can provide, telling us something about the nature of the mining that once took place at Lowick – a vanished industry and largely forgotten element in the history of the village.

The village of Lowick appears today, as a peaceful agricultural community, positioned on a ridge facing Berwick and the Scottish border with the North Sea visible to the east and a view of the Cheviots to the south west. You have to look closely to find any reminders of an industrial past, the suggestion that this particular village was ever anything other than a purely farming community.

Then, as you look more closely, this linear village seems larger than other purely agricultural communities nearby, for although some way distant from the nearest industrial centres around Tyneside, Lowick became caught up in the profound changes associated with the Industrial Revolution, for the village is situated on the Scremerston coal measures, with mining developing in this area from the beginning of the 9th century, providing the means of combustion for the important lime industry, supplying fertiliser for agricultural purposes.

Unlike political revolution with its armed struggle and constitutional changes, the Industrial Revolution transformed communities, manufacturing and extraction processes sweeping in like the tide, changing the pattern of village life fixed for centuries, before withdrawing again, as the mines close, the industry disappears. Left behind, like so much flotsam, are the different elements from this former existence, buildings and other features associated with the industrial period, evidence for a different period and way of life

Here in Lowick, the evidence takes the form of an excessive number of former public houses and churches, (five of each) administering to the diverse social and spiritual needs of the community of the time, the names and tendencies reflecting different faiths, occupations and fancies: the Black Bull, the White Swan, the Plough, the Golden Fleece and the Commercial Inn. Then the chapels and churches: St John the Baptist for Anglicans, various Methodist and Presbyterian churches, a Plymouth Brethren Meeting House and finally, the Catholic Church, St Edwards, pointing to the influx of a labouring population migrating to the village to participate in the industrial developments and the new employment opportunities they created. The population of Lowick almost doubled over the fifty-year period from 1811 to 1861 to 1,946 adult inhabitants before falling back sharply to just 877 by 1931.

Kelly's Directory for 1895 describes the village towards the end of the industrial period as 'a long and irregular street of detached houses many of which are thatched and of humble appearance' with the remark that 'coal pits and stone quarries abound here, lime is also burnt in the neighbourhood'.

However, the directory was already out of date, perhaps transcribing earlier descriptions, for in the same year of 1895, Lowick is described in a solicitor's letter (valuing the White Swan Inn at £400) as a 'decaying place … the chief industry lime burning has entirely stopped owing to the failure of the coal supply.' A photograph from the period shows a destitute looking Main Street with a vandalised lamp. The industrial ambitions of the community – which had once extended to the proposal to bring a branch line up from the east coast main-line railway at Beal, four miles to the south – instantly disappear.

It seems important that a period which marked communities in the North East so strongly and over such a long period of time, should not be forgotten, that those surviving features directly associated with the Industrial Revolution should be recognised, helping, through the narrative they provide, to act as memorials for this period of innovation, invention and industrialisation.

The miner's shovel provides an example of this, an image of how things once were, a particular local narrative associated with mining. It is worth noticing that to remove the shovel to a museum would make it lose some of its significance because the value it represents is most important for the community from which it originates.

There are of course other much larger and more visible features in a community that can be directly linked to an industrial past and have the potential to make more effective monuments: the buildings, pathways, bridges and former agricultural and industrial sites.

Surviving elements of this kind could be seen as 'significant local heritage features', features that help link communities to their historic past, giving each one a particular, distinctive character. Their significance, as we have seen with the miner's shovel, possibly did not extend beyond community boundaries.

The lime kiln (left) just outside the village of Lowick has the potential to become a heritage feature of this kind. A solid impressive structure that has something of the visible presence, the solid fortified statement, of a medieval castle. A potential significant local heritage feature, one that needs to be protected and conserved.

With the development of the site around the lime kiln by clearing the scrub, providing good access from the road, benches and information boards, people can sit and contemplate what happened here, the industrial processes associated with this place and the mining and lime burning that took place here, an important reminder of a vanished industrial legacy.

John Daniels

Lowick c.1890.

Lead and Silver

The primary source of lead ore (galena) in North East England is the area known as the North Pennine Orefield, or by geologists as the 'Alston Block', an elevated plateau of about 650 square miles in the west of our region. Much of the Alston Block lies between 700 feet and over 2,000 feet above mean sea level, with more than twenty summits in excess of 2,000 feet – it has the largest continuous areas of land in Britain above 2,000 feet apart from the Scottish Highlands. Its highest point is Cross Fell, once thought to be the highest mountain in England. The population of the area is mainly located in the valleys, but often at altitudes rarely met with elsewhere in the British Isles; Alston is not, however, the highest market town in England – it shares that distinction with Buxton in Derbyshire, another lead-mining area.

It seems probable that the Romans mined lead ore in the North Pennines, but there is only circumstantial evidence to support that notion. In the second half of the 7th century, according to Bede, Lindisfarne thatch was replaced with lead sheet, and the walls of the church were similarly clad, but the source of that lead is unknown, for we only have proof positive of lead ore mining in the north of England from documents dated 1130, which refer to a 'silver mine' on Alston moor, which supplied a mint at Carlisle. Silver is found in varying proportions in many lead ores, and the process of extracting it was known as 'refining'. It has been suggested that the North Pennine Orefield gave Britain its 12th century dominance in world silver production. Thereafter, there are only sporadic written references to lead/silver mining for the Alston Moor area until the 15th century, by which time the lead/silver industry seems to have been a well-established and important regional industry – and a significant wealth producer. It dictated the economy of the North Pennine Orefield for the next three or four centuries.

Towards the end of the 17th century, two major concerns began to co-ordinate and dominate what had earlier been fairly sporadic activity on the orefield. The Allendale Estate was acquired by Sir William Blackett in 1694, and that was the beginning of the company known as 'W B Lead' which mined and smelted ores from its own mines and others in Weardale. Just two years earlier, in 1692, a Quaker company, which would later be known as the London Lead Company, was formed in Bristol, and by 1697 it had spawned the Ryton Smelting Company to smelt and refine ores from Alston Moor at Blaydon on Tyne. Also of significance in a rationalisation of the industry was the award by government of the Derwentwater Estates, which included Alston Moor, to the Commissioners of the Greenwich Hospital for Seamen; they mainly leased out their royalties to the London Lead Company. Thereafter, although other smaller concerns continued to work in the North Pennine Orefield, the area and the industry came to be largely controlled by the Greenwich Hospital/London Lead Company alliance, and W B Lead. And while these organisations were decidedly commercial rivals, they did sometimes work in concert, for example, in road building programmes.

The production of lead from Alston Moor would increase from around 1,000 tons per annum in the late 17th century to 7,500 tons per annum by the 1790s, such that lead may sometimes have been as important as coal in the region's economy, for it had become a commodity of international importance with, for example, Danish shipments of lead from the Tyne to China. Moreover, the region was becoming the country's leading supplier of lead, producing up to forty per cent of UK lead output at certain periods of the 19th century.

For centuries lead ore and other minerals had been extracted from open-cuts, (rather like linear quarries), 'hushes' (technically known as hydraulic opencuts), levels and shafts. Washing and dressing – the separating out of galena from dross – was historically performed by hand on site, and smelting was generally carried out in mills either close to the lead mines (as at Allenheads) or nearer coal mines (as at Dukesfield), their locations usually governed by the availability of water, fuel, and convenient transport routes to the Tyne, the main port of export. The transport by packhorse of ore to the mills, and lead to Tyneside, may have seemed primitive, but for centuries it was suited to the task.

Despite perpetual struggles against underground water, the industry prospered, and witnessed a number of improvements over time: the gradual mechanisation of the washing and dressing procedures, the introduction of better techniques at the smelt mills, and improvements in transport brought about firstly by better roads, mainly turnpikes, and later by railways. One great technological and economic breakthrough was in the process of the desilverisation of lead. Hugh (Lee) Pattinson was born at Alston in 1796, and in or about 1825 he became 'Assay Master' for the Greenwich Hospital, with responsibility for checking the effectiveness of the smelting operations at its smelt mill at Langley on Tyne; by 1829, he was publishing articles on metallurgy and geology. In an attempt to obtain lead in 'powder form' in that year, Pattinson stirred molten lead in a crucible, and noticed that as it cooled, crystal-like particles of lead formed on the cooling surface, and that the molten lead beneath the surface was much richer in silver than the crystallised lead particles. In this simple experiment lay the germ of an improved method for the desilverising of lead. It must have been a eureka moment for Pattinson, but it would be a while before he could realise its full potential. In his own words, 'It was not until the Spring of the year 1833 that [I] was conveniently circumstanced to proceed in applying to practise the principle [I] had developed'. Pattinson had been appointed Chief Agent for the W B Lead smelt mills and its Blaydon refinery in 1832, being based at the latter place, but travelling widely within Alston Moor. One of his first priorities was to deal with difficulties that W B Lead was experiencing in selling its 'Common Lead' that which was deemed not to be worth refining – for it was too 'hard', and plumbers did not like it. He knew that lead could be 'softened' by removing 'impurities', and consequently he returned to his simple experiment at Alston, soon realising that if he could make it economically worthwhile to desilverise common lead, the resultant refined lead would be 'soft', and would sell. From these thoughts and experiments came the 'Pattinson Desilverising Process' of 1833, and whereas formerly it had only been worth refining from ores that would produce more than six ounces of silver per ton of pig lead, the new process was technically and economically viable down to two ounces per ton. W B Lead was not, of course, interested in 'pure research', but Pattinson received the company's backing because it had an economic interest in the possible outcome of Pattinson's experiments; W B Lead was interested in increased profits, and Pattinson himself would not be immune from thoughts of personal pecuniary gain. One,

Left: *Lead miners at Coalcleugh.* Below right: *Conservation and reconstruction at Nenthead.* Bottom: *Elswick Lead Works c.1900, the shot tower survived until the late 1960s.*

possibly unanticipated, result of his new refining technique was that it enabled some abandoned mines and veins to be profitably re-opened by virtue of the silver that could now be recovered. Pattinson's process was a great success and was widely adopted both at home and abroad. By 1873, various Tyneside lead works were, between them, producing about 1.5 million ounces of silver, valued at £400,000 per year.

For all its importance in the lead trade, manufacturers of lead sheet, lead pipe, lead shot, white lead and red lead, were curiously rare on Tyneside before the late 18th century. Indeed, many tons of pig lead had long been carried from Newcastle to London, only to be brought back as lead products. Thus, although most smelt mills in the North Pennine Orefield were also involved in silver refining by a process that produced lead oxide (Litharge), it would seem that this was usually, if not always, reduced back to metallic lead. The first Tyneside lead works as such was that of Walker, Ward & Fishwick established at Elswick on the banks of the navigable Tyne in 1778, mainly to manufacture white lead for sale as a paint pigment. By the mid-1780s, the concern was also making red lead, lead shot, milled lead, and rolled lead; by 1802 the company was called Walkers, Parker & Co. – an illustrious name in Tyneside industrial history – and it would come to produce one-third of the national output of white lead. Other lead works would soon follow, including, by 1801, Hind & Co. at Ouseburn, Locke Blackett at Gallowgate, both in Newcastle, and Easterby Hall & Co. at Bill Quay. By 1862, after even more lead works had been established in the area, Tyneside was nationally pre-eminent in that industry.

The industrial progress of the lead works was remarkable, but a great human price was being paid for it, for the business of white lead manufacture was deadly dangerous to its personnel by virtue of the ingestion of white lead powder – easily the most dangerous process in the entire lead industry. Lead works placed their workers in great peril, and it is hard to avoid the conclusion that, as in some other industries, the labour force was regarded as just another factor of production – as long as the workers' wages were paid, the employer-employee relationship was satisfied. Perhaps then it is not surprising that white lead manufacture was exclusively women's work in the 19th century, and that the health problems associated with work in the white lead works were not seriously addressed until the 1880s, and only then because of public outcry over this plainly deadly job. In 1882, the *Newcastle Courant* reported on the death of a woman worker at the Ouseburn Lead Works who had been there for twelve years, and had married just nine days before her death. The Coroner noted that no blame could be attached to the works, for they had 'all the necessary appliances', but he added 'It is a pity that human beings had to work at such dangerous work at all, and that other means could not be devised'. It was, of course, not beyond the wit of humankind to devise 'other means', or appropriate machines, but as long as poor and poorly-paid women were prepared to do the work, nothing came cheaper, and there was little incentive to mechanise. However, reformers continued to press their claims, and under a Factories Act of 1898 improved white lead drying stoves were enforced on the manufacturers, dust extractors were made mandatory, and women were prohibited from working in white lead works. This meant that men were now to be exclusively employed in the manufacture of white lead, but in much better conditions than those in which the women had previously laboured, and – surprise, surprise – they were to be better paid. After 1900, the incidence of lead poisoning at the lead works began to decline rapidly.

By that time, however, lead mining and processing in the North Pennine Orefield had almost ended. By the late 19th century some mines had begun to concentrate on alternatives to galena. Settlingstones mine, near Newbrough in Northumberland worked Witherite, and for a while was the only witherite mine in the world. The mines of Teesdale and Lunedale produced Barytes, and those in Weardale worked Fluorspar. The Tyneside Lead Works were able to continue their trades by importing lead from Spain, Greece, Mexico and Australia, and one or two of them lasted well into the 20th century.

Precisely how many lead mines have been operated in the North Pennine Orefield has never been enumerated, but there must have been hundreds, conceivably thousands, and mineral prospecting continues in the area. Hope, as they say, springs eternal, and the anticipation of bonanzas is as strong as it ever was. There is a precedent – Hudgill Mine near Alston.

Early in the 19th century, a vein was being worked at Hudgill by two different companies, but both concerns soon gave up their ventures as useless and hopeless. However, a new company was formed in 1813, and £500 capital was raised to try again. Some 225 tons of ore were raised in 1815, with all the capital expended, but in 1816 the concern paid dividends totalling £1,680, and £7,000 in the following year. By 1822, the dividends paid were £38,000, and some ten years later the mine was closed down. Over seventeen years of operation the venture had realised £320,000 for the partners!

Stafford M. Linsley

Left: *The red lead furnaces.* Right: *St Antony's Lead Works. (Images from A* descriptive account of Newcastle, 1894.)

Iron, Steel and Engineering

The various iron and steel industries of north-east England have sometimes been of national significance, and occasionally of international standing. The extent of such industries in the medieval period has not been fully researched, but it seems not to have been of any great significance. Only one north-eastern blast furnace (for converting iron ore to pig iron) is known to have worked for part of the 16th century – at Wheelbirks, near Stocksfield, c.1570 – and two others for part of the 17th century, Hunwick (1632–c.1689) and Allensford (1670-c.1715): these all used local ores, were charcoal charged, and water powered. None of them appear to have been very long lived, and for most of the 18th century local iron ore was only smelted at Bedlington, possibly at Lee Hall near Bellingham for a short time in the 16th century, at Whitehill, Chester-le-Street, (1745-c.1790), the region's first coke-charged plant), and at Lemington on Tyne (see front cover) towards the end of the century, the latter becoming the North East's first integrated plant, that is taking in ore, coal and limestone for its blast furnaces, and being equipped with a foundry, wrought iron plant, and rolling mills.

There were, however, some internationally renowned 18th century ironworking enterprises in the region, dependent not upon local ores but on imports of the best quality wrought iron, (generally known as 'bar iron'), from Sweden and Russia, as well as pig iron from America. This was the basis of the considerable iron and steel enterprises of the Derwent Valley in County Durham, where the imported irons were reworked to produce manufactured goods, or converted into steel by the cementation process,

to be used for the manufacture of a variety of products including edge tools. At this period the cutlers of Sheffield were pleased to import what they referred to as 'Newcastle Steel'; by 1740, there may have been six cementation furnaces on Tyneside, whereas Sheffield only had two and Birmingham three.

The Swedes were so constantly interested in what entrepreneurs in Britain, and in the North East in particular, were doing with all their iron imports, that several Swedish and other travellers, metallurgists, and industrialists came over to examine the situation, perhaps fearful that further developments in Britain might bring a mutually profitable situation to an end. Hence our knowledge of north-east iron and steel at this time depends very much on the travel diaries of men like Henry Kalmeter, Samuel Schroderstierna, Reinhold Rücker Angerstein and Johan Ludvig Robsahm.

The most famous of the Derwent Valley enterprises was established in the 1690s by Ambrose Crowley, and described in 1770/71 as 'supposed to be among the greatest manufactories of the kind in Europe'. The Crowley works was unique in having a written constitution, the *Law Book of the Crowley Ironworks*, of about 1700. This Law Book was very much ahead of its time in its innovations in industrial welfare, for example in the insurance scheme established to pay for certain social services for the workforce, to which both employer and employees contributed. Thus the Law Book, embodied a series of laws that were not only intended to govern the working practices in the various works, but also to regulate the social order both within and without the concerns: in this

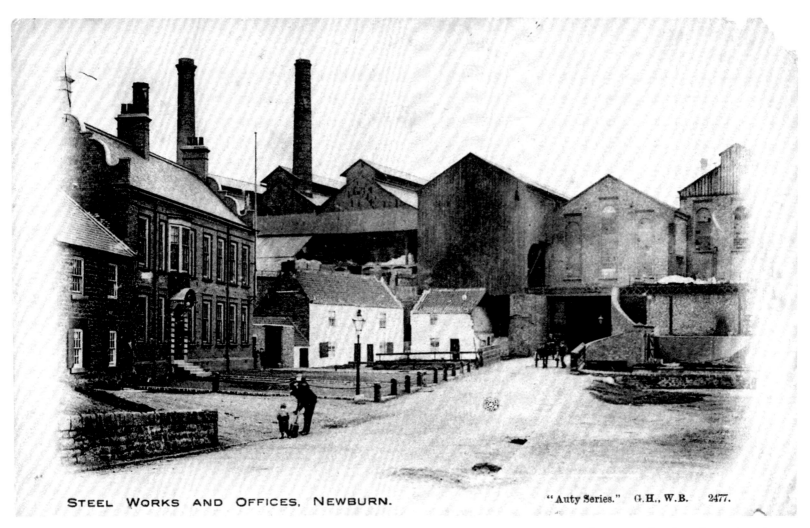

STEEL WORKS AND OFFICES, NEWBURN.

"Auty Series." G.H., W.B. 2477.

Spencer's Steelworks in Newburn

it foreshadowed the efforts of Robert Owen more than a century later. It is a fascinating document and, viewed from today, contains much that we might find enlightening, but also amusing. Thus Order 85 of the Crowley Law Book, entitled 'Extravagancies Discouraged', noted that:

Whereas Mr. Crowley hath made it his observation that morning drinking hath been of fatal consequence to all that have made a practice of it: 1) It is of all things the most destructive to business; 2) It destroyeth health, memory, and understanding; 3) It produceth nothing but folly and madness; 4) It wastes the only time to do business ... it is therefore declared that Mr. Crowley will take effectual care to discharge [sack] all such as shall for the future practise the drinking of any strong liquor before they go to dinner.

And 'Order Number 85', further noted that certain named former employees had:

... all rendered themselves unfit for any business, and reduced themselves into extreme poverty [by] pride ... by gameing ... by sotting and ... by trading ... and in going much abroad, particularly to Newcastle which hath been the ruine of several.

Admiralty contracts probably formed the basis of Crowley's business, but a wide range of goods was produced at the works at Winlaton, Winlaton Mill, and Swalwell, as described by Angerstein in 1754: hoes for the West Indian tobacco plantations, anchors, bolts and crowbars, harpoons and other equipment for whaling, balances and lifting jacks, machetes to cut sugar cane, fire-

The Tyne with Spencer's Steel works and Lemington glass cones seen through the smog, around 1900.

irons, braziers, nails, hammers and other blacksmith's tools, etc. It was, perhaps, the largest commercial organisation in the country, and one of the very first 'factories' anywhere. Moreover, it gave north-east England an international reputation during the 18th century. But by 1825, Mackenzie could write 'The iron manufacturies at Winlaton and Swalwell have greatly declined.' The Crowley firm was still at work, however, under 'Crowley Millington', and although its great days were over, it continued to innovate, introducing crucible steel-making to the North East in 1810.

By the early 19th century, with the Crowley works in decline, Hawks of Gateshead were in an ascendency as an iron and engineering works, the Bedlington ironworks was doing quite well, and John Spencer's Newburn works became of national importance. The latter works had been established at Newburn in 1810, initially to make engineer's files, the associated settlement being known as 'New Sheffield', and it was to become, for a while, the most important steel works of its kind in the North East. Cementation and crucible furnaces were added, puddled steel was made, its early specialty being the production of railway springs and buffers. Other steel concerns continued on a relatively small scale into the 19th century, but the overall situation was soon to change as north-eastern steelmaking became overshadowed by ironmaking: the

North East's pre-eminence in 18th century steel production gradually gave way to a less important but locally based and dispersed iron industry, independent of imported bar irons, but using local coal-measure iron ores, plus ironstone nodule deposits of the 'Mountain Limestone' areas of Northumberland, and ore deposits in Weardale.

For the first few decades of the century only the Lemington works had blast furnaces in action in the region, although several iron forges remained quite vibrant. The Industrial Revolution was forged in iron, and as the century progressed, very few workable ore deposits were to remain unworked. Boulton & Watt blowing engines lessened the need for water power and increased the desirability of associated coal and ironstone supplies. Consequently, several works were established in the 1830s, a time when north-east demand for iron was rising, and the result, locally, was a very scattered industry. Coke-charged blast furnace sites, mainly using local ironstones, were established at Walker (1827), Birtley (1828), Wylam (1836), Bellingham (1836), Ridsdale (1836), Stanhope (1840), Tow Law (1840), Brinkburn (c.1845), Haltwhistle (c.1845), Consett (1842), Witton Park (1846), and Elswick, Newcastle (1860). Most were quite modest affairs except, notably, that at Consett, and all but Consett were ultimately doomed. At the beginning of the 1840s, the north east of England was, in any national context, a relatively insignificant producer of pig iron, but by 1865 the region was producing some twenty-one per cent of the nation's output. How did this come about?

Although more iron-making plants were to be established in various parts of Northumberland and Durham in the second half of the 19th century, as at as at Tudhoe, Felling, Washington, Haltwhistle, Ferryhill, and Seaham, the industry's growth thereafter was to be dominated by the emergent Cleveland iron industry, and the consequent decline of most other ironworks within the region.

After early discouraging experiments with ores from Cleveland, (which had been tried in small parcels with indifferent results over several decades), furnaces were built at Walker on Tyne in 1842 to utilise precisely those ores. The massive exploitation of the Cleveland deposits which was to follow, combined with the growing use of South Durham coke and Weardale limestone, led to the gradual abandonment of all of the above named ironworks except that at Consett, and to the concurrent concentration of the industry on Teesside. In 1854 the production of pig iron in the Cleveland District was only 250,000 tons, but it produced 1,968,972 tons in 1872. Its share in national output increased from seventeen per cent in 1860 to thirty-two per cent in 1875, by which time the district had become the biggest single iron producing area in the world. Its growth since 1850 had been remarkable even by 19th century standards, its rise to prominence having been masterminded by incoming entrepreneurs and engineers, mainly self-made men rather than hereditary landowners. The population of Middlesbrough grew from one-hundred and fifty in 1831 to 104,000 by 1911, a dramatic rise fuelled by immigration – skilled ironworkers from Wales and Lancashire, and unskilled workers from agriculture and Ireland. Little wonder that Chancellor of the Exchequer W. E. Gladstone, on a visit to Middlesbrough 1862, described the town as 'This remarkable place, the youngest child of England's enterprise ... It is an infant, gentlemen, but it is an infant Hercules.' Even so, it was not without significance that, in 1868, the Iron and Steel Institute was formally inaugurated in Newcastle, a token of the region's 19th century role in that industry.

Mechanical engineering

Some local ironworks manufactured finished products needed by local trades, and it was from such work that mechanical engineering emerged in the North East. It has been argued that mechanical engineering was born with the Newcomen Engine of 1712, and although this ignores the centuries of millwrighting that preceded it, the rapid acceptance of this engine in the north east coalfield demonstrates a desire to assimilate advanced engineering techniques and to widen engineering expertise. Indeed the north-easterner Henry Beighton is usually credited with perfecting the engine's valve control gear in 1718, while another local engineer, William Brown of Throckley, (c.1720-1782) seems to have built, on average, one Newcomen engine per year during his adult life. The first workable rotative steam engine was due to Joseph Oxley, the Delaval Agent at Hartley and, significantly, James Watt saw this engine at work in 1768 before going on to produce his own much more effective rotative engine. It was from an accumulating expertise arising out of the coal and shipbuilding industries that some of the region's most important engineering firms sprang.

Although some iron founders and engineers were in evidence in the 18th century, most of the important engineering firms had not yet come into being. But Murray & Co. of Chester-le-Street, established in 1793, were followed by enterprises such as Losh, Wilson & Bell (Walker 1807), R. & W. Hawthorn (Newcastle 1817), R. Stephenson & Co. (Newcastle 1823 – the world's first locomotive-building factory), Gilkes Wilson & Co. (Middlesbrough 1844), W. G. Armstrong & Co. (Newcastle upon Tyne 1847), Clarke, Chapman & Co. (originally formed by William Clarke in 1864; in 1882 they employed women as draughtsmen, one of the first concerns nationally to do so). Whilst the pattern for the engineering industry was set in the early years of the 19th century, it continued to expand and diversify right to the end of that century, in particular with Charles Parsons's pioneering work on steam turbines for marine propulsion and for electricity generation – a fusion of mechanical and electrical engineering.

Marine engineering

It is hardly surprising that north-east England should become intimately involved in maritime industries. Shipbuilding is dealt with elsewhere in this book, but it is perhaps worth noting here that a number of north-eastern shipbuilders, and some specialist firms, undertook ship repair work, while a few companies specialised in shipbreaking. Moreover, steam propulsion for ships gave birth to marine engineering, and the Newcastle firm of R. & W. Hawthorn regularly manufactured marine engines from the 1820s, later supplying such engines for colliers built by Palmers of Hebburn. Some shipbuilders, like Doxford's on the Wear, engined their own ships, but specialist marine engine firms also developed. One such was the North Eastern Marine Engineering Company, founded in 1854, the builder of the region's first triple-expansion steam engine in 1882. Likewise, the first quadruple-expansion engine to find commercial use anywhere, was built at West Hartlepool in 1894. In the same year, on Tyneside, Charles Parsons established the Marine Steam Turbine Company Ltd., and after his tiny ship *Turbinia* had steamed rings around the assembled fleet at the 1897 Spithead Review in a brilliantly audacious manner, the future of turbine propulsion was assured. North East shipbuilding and marine engineering moved into the twentieth century with appropriate optimism.

Numerous lesser industries supported shipbuilding – a point evident in the 1851 census returns for Sunderland for example, which numbered amongst its total male population of 30,000, some 2,000 shipwrights, eighty-two boat builders, 784 joiners, 235 painters, ninety-nine anchor smiths, 479 blacksmiths, 216 ropemakers and 118 sailcloth makers. Whilst some of these would not be involved with shipping requirements, the majority almost certainly were. In spite of the development of machine-made 'patent' rope, first produced in Sunderland in 1797, which theoretically removed the need for traditional rope walks, handmade rope continued to be preferred in many shipyards for decades thereafter.

Local engineers and ironworks also played an important role in bridge building. The 1796 cast-iron bridge at Sunderland had more than double the span of the earlier bridge at Ironbridge, and until its replacement in 1929 it remained the largest cast-iron bridge in the country. Europe's earliest known permanent suspension bridge, a footbridge of 1741, spanned the Tees at Holwick, and its first suspension bridge for vehicular traffic crossed the Tweed near Horncliffe in 1821: this latter bridge, although subsequently strengthened, retains its original towers and wrought-iron chain links, and is now the oldest surviving suspension bridge in the world still carrying vehicular traffic. Its 437ft span was much larger than any then-existing span of any sort in Western Europe. Another virtually unaltered suspension bridge, complete with toll house, is at Whorlton in County Durham, built by the Newcastle architect John Green in 1831: the bridge is still supported only by its original chains, making it unique amongst early British suspension bridges. Green later introduced laminated-timber bridge construction to this country and although his viaducts at Ouseburn and Willington for the Newcastle & North Shields Railway were later rebuilt in wrought iron, they retain the overall form of the original timber structures. The railway age of course offered many challenges to the nation's bridge engineers, and two of Robert Stephenson's finest bridges, the Royal Border over the Tweed, and the High Level over the Tyne (for which some of the iron mixture came from Ridsdale in Northumberland, while the ironwork was supplied by three local companies), demonstrate how he was prepared to use a standard form for the first but an innovative design for the second where circumstances demanded something special. The High Level Bridge is probably the paramount example of technological imagination realised through excellent iron-founding and iron-forging skills.

The emergence of Teesside's iron industry also fostered the development of bridge-building concerns. As manufacturers of iron in stock, some Teesside ironmasters also came to specialise in fabricated lattice-girder bridges, and Gilkes Wilson & Co., who had earlier manufactured steam engines, came to concentrate on bridges to Thomas Bouch's designs, as Hopkins Gilkes & Co. They supplied his spectacular viaducts for the South Durham & Lancaster Union Railway, but also his spectacularly unsuccessful Tay Bridge. In similar vein, Head Wrightson of Teesside became the country's major builders of pleasure piers and their work can be seen around our coasts.

W. G. Armstrong's Tyne Swing Bridge of 1876 was the largest such in the world at the time of its opening, and the firm became the predominant supplier of moveable bridges in the country, including the machinery for Tower Bridge in London. But several other notable moveable bridges were built in the region including the Middlesbrough Transporter (1910-11, designed by Cleveland Bridge Engineering Co.), the Newport (Tees) Lift Bridge, (1931–34, designed by Mott, Hay & Anderson, and constructed by Dorman Long & Co., and at the time, the largest vertical-lift bridge in the world), and the Aluminum Bascule Bridge of 1948 in the Sunderland docks area by Head Wrightson of Stockton. The latter was described as an 'epoch-making development' as the world's first aluminium alloy bascule bridge, but seemingly it was also the last such, and was demolished in 1978/9.

Engineers

The region clearly possessed the economic and material resources needed to develop its engineering industries, and in this environment talented engineers like George and Robert Stephenson, W. G. Armstrong, Percy G. B. Westmacott, Lowthian Bell and Jeremiah Head, all of whom became presidents of the Institution of Mechanical Engineers, provided the intellectual capital that would influence the nation's destiny. And for every Stephenson there were others like William Walker, born in Houghton-le-Spring in 1830 and apprenticed at Thornley Colliery, but later to be awarded a gold medal by the Indian Agricultural Congress for his design and construction of sugar beet factories, coffee works, and an iron lighthouse. Or like John Dixon, born in Newcastle and educated at Bruce's Academy, who, after an apprenticeship with R. Stephenson & Co, followed by spells with the Consett Iron Co. and the Bedlington ironworks, went on to become a civil engineer of international importance. Amongst Dixon's commissions were a bridge over the Nile at Cairo, piers in Mexico, and a sanitary works in Rio de Janeiro. He went on to lay the first railway in China and subsequently to re-erect Cleopatra's Needle on the Victoria Embankment, London. Little wonder that William Fairbairn, another great 19th century engineer, regarded his apprenticeship at a North East colliery as probably the most important influence on his personal development.

On the other hand, William Armstrong had no professional background in engineering. He was a Newcastle solicitor who dabbled in electrostatics and hydraulics before embarking on the engineering business that was to make him the 'father of hydraulic engineering' and much else. His Elswick works were about three miles upriver of Newcastle's old stone arch bridge, a factor clearly not seen to be of much importance when the works was commenced, yet it was not until that bridge was replaced by the hydraulically powered Swing Bridge, designed and created by Armstrong's, that the works could really expand the armaments side of its production and to introduce shipbuilding. Eventually even the clearance afforded by the new swing bridge was inadequate for newly built ships to pass, and this forced shipbuilding at Elswick to be transferred to downstream Walker on Tyne. As Armstrong's works grew to massive proportions so the former green fields around them were filled with row upon row of terraced housing, mainly of the Tyneside flat variety, serviced by schools, chapels, washhouses and of course public houses such as The Hydraulic Crane, The Forge Hammer, The Moulders' Arms, and The Crooked Billet, the latter name, interestingly enough, predating the works. The works had begun with a workforce of some twenty or thirty men, but by the end of the century it probably numbered tens of thousands.

Stafford M. Linsley

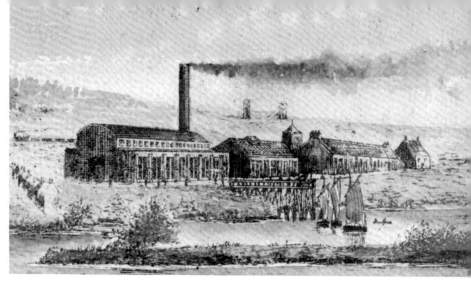

Clockwise from top left: 1) *The Swing Bridge under construction c.1875.*
2) *A sketch of Elswick Engine Works, 1847, note the islands in the Tyne.*
3) *An 1887 'bird's-eye view' of Elswick Shipyard, Steelworks and Engine Works*